Caring and

Physical Education, Therapy
and
Sherborne Developmental Movement

Edited by John Dibbo and Sue Gerry

Acknowledgements: John and Sue would like to recognise the support of the UK Sherborne Foundation in the setting up of the Conference and to dedicate this book to Bill Richards who has been the inspiration behind introducing Sherborne Developmental Movement to the Physical Education degree at Rolle.

Contents

Chapter 1 - Introduction

Movement - Caring and Sharing
The Sherborne Way

John Dibbo & Sue Gerry

It may be useful to begin by explaining the purpose of the first International Conference on Sherborne Developmental Movement (SDM). Firstly, the underlying philosophy of the BEd Physical Education course at the University of Plymouth has a person centred approach operating within a reflexive framework. This approach to teaching is, we believe, an appropriate way to prepare teachers for a career in primary education with a specialist interest in Physical Education. We have found SDM to be one way of enabling students to reach an understanding that movement has the potential to develop more than just the physical aspect of Physical Education. Secondly, conversations with colleagues using SDM in other fields also suggest that this method contributes to the development of the whole person. So, we were pleased to bring together teachers, therapists and researchers from Europe and Scandinavia for the first time to share their expertise, experience and research findings. The Conference papers presented in this book show the links across a range of academic disciplines. We identified a dominant theme from the conference as a developing humanistic perspective evident in the thinking and writing of people from different cultures and disciplines. The two sections of the book present both the academic debate behind Veronica Sherborne's philosophy and case study material showing the application of her work. This chapter briefly describes the origin of SDM and identifies how the range of work currently taking place across Europe sustains and develops the work begun by Veronica Sherborne.

The idea of developmental movement teaching introduced by Veronica Sherborne was influenced by her background in Physical Education and physiotherapy. She was strongly influenced through her knowledge of the work of Rudolf Laban who believed that movement was central to life. Sherborne's initial philosophies and practical ideas were directed towards the field of mental handicap and from this base she established an international reputation. However, in the last six years the scope of her work has widened having a growing influence on the personal development of all ages from infancy to maturity. This included teaching in mainstream education, special education and work with parents and other professionals. Until her death in 1990 she was one of the true innovators within the field of movement education. She published her only book in 1990: Developmental Movement for Children in which she clearly indicated her developing philosophy and provided examples and discussion of the application of her work.

The phrase 'developmental movement' was not lightly chosen by Veronica as it reflects her journey of discovery about relationships through movement. She refined her understanding through considerable teaching experience, thought and discussion which can be described as a reflexive approach to her work. It is this particular quality that many see as paramount in her approach and one that leads the search towards better practice.

SDM is now being more widely applied in education from mainstream to special needs and in physiotherapy and occupational therapy situations. Those who are influenced by her work believe that for the learner or the patient SDM provides a sound basis for the development of body awareness, positive self concept and relationships. For the teacher it locates the physical experience of Physical Education within an holistic framework by providing a range of movement activities that require thought and care. Thought in the sense that the child can

1

interpret and develop the physical skills to his level of ability within a caring and safe environment. The caring and safe environment is also created through developing a sense of awareness for others by enabling children and adults to work together in partnership activities. For the therapist it provides a secure framework of movement that can help the patient overcome some of the difficulties he may face.

In Chapter 2 Bill Richards, a founder member of Sherborne Foundation UK, describes the application of SDM with mainstream and special needs children in primary education. He discusses the extent to which SDM is a central or peripheral strategy to caring and sharing, teaching and learning. He explores the possible reasons for such a diversity of influence, with particular reference to the physical curriculum in primary education. He also examines the relationship of SDM to alternative movement forms; to the Halliwick method of swimming developed by James McMillan and to Conductive Education developed by Professor Andras Peto. In essence he seeks to argue for a place where SDM is at the centre and not the periphery of the educative process.

The way forward with Veronica's work is discussed by Maureen Douglas, a Senior Lecturer at the University of Plymouth, UK, in Chapter 3. She contextualises Sherborne by reference to two somatic thinkers, Delsarte and Laban. She suggests that Sherborne is part of a continuum involved in shifting the focus of movement practice from the arts to education and therapy. Having reflected on the essential features of SDM she considers its uniqueness as the combination of developmentally appropriate movement experience linked to relationship play.

Sue Gerry, writing in Chapter 4, looks at Health Focussed Physical Education in primary schools in the UK. She develops the debate with a consideration of well-being within the Physical Education environment. Here the traditional methods of testing, measuring and quantifying health and fitness can threaten the child's self image. Her findings based on conversations with children show how they felt threatened by these traditional approaches. By adopting and adapting SDM some of the children's fears are reduced. These ways of working do not replace traditional methods but provide a platform of self-confidence to enable the children to handle the more risky images of the self portrayed in the Health and Fitness testing arena. Again, this is a more holistic approach which she argues contributes to the well-being of children.

A central issue of SDM is the importance of creating a learning environment which gives the child early success and confidence. John Dibbo, who is working with Bill Richards at Rolle in initial teacher training, discusses in Chapter 5 a safe and secure environment which can be offered within Physical Education and SDM where children and adults work together and exercise responsibility through decision making processes. These experiences are delivered within a clearly defined movement framework based on Laban's philosophies. This is a physical experience but it is also cognitive and acknowledges the importance of feelings for the individual alone and for others. Thus, it has the potential to meet the needs of the whole child - the physical, the affective and the cognitive domains operating within a clearly defined movement framework.

Gerrit Loots, a leading psychologist working with SDM in Belgium, examines in Chapter 6 the strategies for supporting parents and their children with disabilities. In 1982 he established an early intervention team to discover ways to stimulate the development of children with special needs during the first years of their life. Very often the child has been the focus for intervention, but Loots presents a programme using SDM involving the whole family working together, enabling the child to manage the problems she faces. He reviews the interactional context of young hearing-impaired children to identify typical communication patterns. Where he identified a barrier to communication he introduced SDM to support the families and help overcome any communication problems.

2

Other research from Germany by Cristian Dirjack measures interaction levels between children and between children and teachers and contributes towards the growing empirical evidence to support the argument that SDM enhances the development of positive relationships. He writes in Chapter 7 about SDM and Games Teaching in schools in Freiburg, Germany and from his research he makes potentially useful pedagogical and clinical recommendations.

In Part 2 of the book a series of case studies are presented which locate SDM firmly within a range of contexts. Vesa Keskitalo (Chapter 8) at the University of Jyvaskyla, Finland presents his current findings on research into progression and continuity in primary school Physical Education in Finland. He is investigating current practice in Physical Education teaching in Finland and has used SDM as a means of challenging and changing current practice. His initial conclusions show the potential of SDM to fulfil this need in a sensitive and caring way.

Post-graduate research being conducted by Steve Mellor (Chapter 9) at the University of Plymouth, UK, shows SDM as an appropriate means of supporting non-specialist physical education teachers in primary schools. He identifies that relationship play and caring and sharing activities of SDM lend themselves to working with individuals and groups of people in new or stressful situations. His findings have confirmed that the use of elements of SDM to underpin undergraduate teaching for the non-specialist teacher of Physical Education at the University of Plymouth are well founded.

Linda Mongey, an undergraduate student working with John Dibbo, writes in Chapter 10 about developing gymnastic competence through SDM. She suggests that a non-threatening learning environment contributes to the children working together sensitively, exercising responsibility, making decisions and therefore having more ownership of their own learning. The research uses the work of Dibbo and Gerry to establish that the body should not be treated from the perspective of an object but needs to be considered as an interrelated whole, the body and mind being one construct inseparable from each other .

Leslie Craigie, of Mossknowe Special School, Glasgow, Scotland, links aspects of SDM with the work of The Scottish Council for Movement Therapy in Chapter 11. The Council have been active in developing a non-verbal form of communication which is used with those who suffer blocks in their language and communication systems. Movement therapy uses the mother-infant model as a basis for the development of this work, involving turn-taking or synchronous patterns of movement where the adult tries to fit into the child's style of behaviour. Movement therapists focus primarily on searching for ways which help the child explore her feelings and express her emotions in a carefully constructed and safe place. This is achieved through imitation and 'fitting in' techniques before entering the intimate world of holding, rocking, rolling, lifting and swinging activities through SDM.

Drama Consultant and ex-head of Drama at St Andrew's College of Education, Glasgow, Scotland, Irene Rankin, illustrates the effective application of SDM within a drama context, again with children who have learning difficulties in Chapter 12. In her story "A Quest for the Sun" she shows how SDM could be used to help the adults (teachers and helpers) communicate their feelings and emotions to the children. The sequencing and repetition of events combine to encourage involvement and concentration from the children. "A Quest for the Sun" is a story written by Irene which allows the children to interpret movement experiences through drama and language.

Undergraduates Linda Sired and Kathryn Firth investigate the application of SDM in a group of primary schools in Devon, UK, which have units to support children with learning difficulties. The specific focus of this research considers the relationship between language development and movement experience for children with special educational needs. The students present a case study in Chapter 13 which indicates strong positive links between language development and SDM. This is an extension of the research established by Bill

Richards who is involved in considerable teaching with children with special needs in Physical Education.

The value of SDM has been more formally recognised in Belgium. A Developmental Movement Programme in Special Education provision was established in September 1992, funded by the Flemish Federal Education Department. In Chapter 14 Rita Vermeesch, a physiotherapist and Willy Dewinter, a teacher, working in Special Education and well experienced in SDM, describe how they have introduced the method into more than 38 Primary and Secondary Schools for mentally and physically handicapped children in Flanders. Through movement sessions in the schools this work has concentrated on developing a positive atmosphere where the socio-emotional development of the children is given equal importance with the cognitive domain.

SDM can be linked with the best thinking and practice when looking at the different needs of people in a variety of circumstances. This situation is reflected on by Janet Sparkes, a Senior Lecturer of Physical Education at King Alfred's College, Winchester, UK, as she describes how she uses SDM as a way of contributing to personal change with institutionalised children in a Romanian orphanage in Chapter 15. The children in their formative years had been deprived of those facets of stimulation recognised as essential in the course of human development. In an emotional yet sensitive presentation, Janet describes the living conditions of these children as clearly lacking in any form of sensory stimulation. She writes that the children exist amongst others but that there is very little evidence of these children acknowledging each other's presence. Equally, there is little evidence of play and a lack of recognition of their needs by their carers. In this environment she introduced an SDM programme which gave the children a sense of their physical well-being, which created an environment where co-operative activity was uppermost, which developed individual qualities and which gave children access to success and non-judgemental teaching.

Peter Bruckenwell, a Senior Occupational Therapist in the UK, describes his work with children who have profound and multiple learning difficulties in Chapter 16. He talks about his role as facilitator where he strives to create a shared dialogue of touch and movement between himself and those with whom he works. SDM is one of a range of strategies employed in his work as well as elements of The Van Dijk Approach, Body Mind Centring and Contact Improvisation.

In their different ways the readings in this book show the value of looking at SDM from a range of standpoints showing the common ground accessible to us all. Perhaps the greatest benefit is that the chapters concentrate on what users of SDM actually do and their thinking behind their doing. The Conference was an attempt to bring together a wide variety of people who use SDM for the purpose of discussing the common ground and debating the academic and philosophical basis of this common ground.

Part One

The Academic Framework

Chapter 2

Sherborne Developmental Movement
Central or Peripheral

Bill Richards

I had been working in different contexts with Sherborne Developmental Movement (SDM) for about 13 years before I really began to appreciate and understand much of its undoubted significance to so many people. This may appear to be a strange statement but in many ways is closely related to the death of Veronica in 1990 and the evident need to present a reasoned justification for this form of movement at a time when such an outstanding practitioner was no longer with us. It was also at a time of considerable educational change as a result of the Education Reform Act of 1988 with an increased effort being made by the government to exercise influence over curriculum content.

The challenge to develop and articulate a theoretical framework that would help to strengthen the place of SDM was accepted because of a real belief in the value of such experience for all people irrespective of age, ability or background. From my experience with SDM in mainstream education, special education, the youth service and a young offenders project I identified common ground with the developmental group work of Leslie Button (1976) and the new games approach of Terry Orlick (1978). SDM worked in a variety of settings and with a variety of people, the mentally ill, management training and work in sub-normality hospitals.

More recently in my journey, my thoughts have been further reinforced as I have gained experience in the work of James McMillan with the Halliwick Swimming method and Professor Andras Peto with conductive education. As with Sherborne both these innovators developed a form of movement that initially was specific to a particular population. James McMillan began his work in 1949 at the Halliwick School for girls in Southgate, London where he developed a method of teaching the physically handicapped to swim based on known scientific principles of hydrodynamics and body mechanics. Swimmers are taught on a one to one basis of swimmer and instructor until complete independence is achieved.

> The swimmer instructor pair becomes a unit within a group activity so that the swimmer gains the advantages of social interaction with his peers while at the same time enjoying the unobtrusive but constant attention of an individual instructor. Through the medium of games appropriate to their age and ability, groups are made aware of the properties and behaviour of water and how to control their own specific balance problems.
> Physiotherapy : October 1981 Vol. 67, No 10.

McMillan clearly supports the notion of the importance of developing relationships which lead his physically handicapped population to a form of body management in the environment of water. Sherborne (1990) has similar beliefs in the construction of movement experiences because she concludes that children have two basic needs 'they need to feel at home in their own bodies and so gain body mastery, and they need to be able to form relationships' (p. v). 'The work of Professor Peto has been concerned with the orthofunctional re-establishment of forms of disorganisation of the human functions in particular those with motor handicaps' (Hary 1988).

Most of what we do involves the co-ordination of a variety of movements to create complex functions such as the manipulation of objects, speaking etc. A deficit in movement potential can have a significant effect on the development of these functions. This relationship between movement and learning has considerable support, for example Alice Yardley (1972) believes that:

> Movement makes life what it is. Without movement there would be no life. Basic to living is the process of learning and without movement no learning takes place.

Conductive Education seeks to re-establish a communication system between the mind and body in children with motor disorders helping maximise their learning potential. Fundamental to this process is the belief that learning is much more than the mechanical copying of an action. Peto attempts to reconstruct the implicit content of an action by more than merely adding together the fragments of the action.

> It must be possible for one to anticipate the ultimate aim of the action, motivated by the importance that it represents and because of this it is not sufficient only to look and hear. Thus learning to understand and to function is no small matter. Mere copying would be a trivial and sad business (Hary 1988).

Sherborne also counselled against the mechanical moving of a handicapped child. The child certainly needs movement stimulation to help in the recognition that they have a body. The link between movement and other learning experiences is clear but as Sherborne believes:

> It is important not to move the child mechanically, but to make the experience as enjoyable as possible, making the learning a play situation (Sherborne 1990 p.39).

I believe there are similarities in the underlying philosophies and in the teaching and learning constructs between Sherborne, McMillan and Peto to which I shall return later in this chapter. I propose a theoretical construct that seeks to clarify this rather confused thinking. What follows is not a tight framework from a research led academic perspective but an attempt to begin the process from an experiential level and to argue that Sherborne should be a central rather than peripheral experience.

Sherborne's background in physiotherapy and Physical Education helped her to develop an openness in accepting movement principles from these complementary areas. The development of her work preceded the Warnock Report (1978) but was firmly grounded in one of the principles expressed in this report. Warnock felt that special schools could be a valuable theoretical and pedagogical support for teachers in mainstream schools working with youngsters with some form of learning difficulty. Indeed, in large schools, the report envisaged some form of resource centre where visiting specialist teachers may work with children. The report emphasised the need to reduce the professional isolation that can occur in special schools and recommended 'the development of some special schools as training bases' (p. 255).

Inter-professional co-operation using the relevant strengths of the various branches of education and the support services to develop a coherent and unified approach to teaching and learning is, in my view, far from being realised. Warnock (1978) addressed the area of inter-professional training and recommended:

> That there should be an expansion of the provision of short courses of inter-professional training which focus on subjects of common concern to members of different professions (p. 301).

How far can we claim to have moved in the intervening 16 years? Perhaps not far enough from either a theoretical or pedagogical perspective. I believe SDM can and in practice does offer a movement form encapsulating this inter-professional dimension. SDM draws from the therapeutic, psychological and educational perspectives - a form of movement ahead of its time. It has always been acknowledged, and certainly by Sherborne (1990), that Rudolf Laban helped to provide the framework for the development of this movement form.

> There are many of us who owe a great debt to Laban and his work...Laban's aim was not so much to make successful performers as to develop the personality, to develop potential, and to help people to understand and experience the widest range of movement possible (p.v).

The vocabulary of movement she developed, whilst initially recognising the needs of the mentally handicapped, was firmly constructed around the body, spatial, qualitative and relationship dimensions offered by Laban. The teaching of movement has been strongly influenced by Rudolf Laban and his contribution to movement education in this country is accepted as a major one. From such a base Sherborne's work has been developed by some practitioners as an integral part of an approach to the physical curriculum. Sherborne felt that she focused on developing general skills in accomplishing different aspects of movement which could then be adapted and applied to different physical tasks. It is clear that through her understanding of Laban's principles there are recognisable links with expressive forms of movement such as dance. Work is currently in progress to explore SDM as a basis for gymnastic development[1]. The idea of SDM helping to facilitate movement confidence will be explored more deeply later in the chapter. However, implicit within SDM is the development of self, having a direct relationship to successful outcomes in both the movement areas of dance and gymnastics. It is no less significant in the movement field of games where the construction of positive relationships is often held to be fundamental to success. In fact the government, again in an effort to exercise some control over the physical curriculum, argue that all secondary schools should be required to teach team games. The dominant ideologies which promote the character building qualities of competitive sport were evident in a recent newspaper article (The Times 8/4/94) advocating 'the virtues of winning modestly and losing gracefully'. As such, the government have placed the movement areas of dance, gymnastics and games firmly at the heart of the physical curriculum for primary children. Sir Ron Dearing was charged with providing advice on a revised National Curriculum in England. The Physical Education Advisory Group recommend these areas as the core for children in Key Stage 1 with continued development through Key Stage 2 (Dearing Report 1994).

Earlier the observation was made that some practitioners use SDM as an integral component of an approach to the physical curriculum but, I argue, that the approach is still largely peripheral in the area of Physical Education. The emphasis on the core experiences of gymnastics, dance and games has never been more explicitly made than through the NCC orders. SDM can impact on all three of these movement areas as may other movement forms. In the same way as Laban has had a major influence on movement development in this country, Sherborne could have a significant impact on the development of the physical curriculum, centrally rather than peripherally.

Fundamental to this claim is that Sherborne recognises the individual and through movement experiences seeks to enhance the development of that individual. This is far from unique and can rightly be claimed as a central aim by a variety of practitioners in associated fields. It is the understanding of the totality of individual development that begins to both set Sherborne apart and at the same time place her work centrally in any developmental process. I have already suggested that the construction of her work draws from the therapeutic and also the relationship between movement experiences and learning is a rich one. Sherborne (1990) herself refers to:

---

[1] Dibbo and Mongey 1994, unpublished research into SDM and gymnastics

... experiences rather than exercises because they combine both physical and psychological learning experiences (p. vi).

Developmental psychology has been defined by Berk (1991) as:

The field devoted to understanding all changes that human beings experience throughout the life span (p. G-4).

Keogh and Sugden (1985) define development as 'Adaptive change towards competence' (p.6). Sherborne entitled her book "Developmental Movement for Children" capturing that balance of the psychological and physical and although limiting her text to children it is clear from our experience that she could have included ages throughout the entire life span. She clearly understood the needs of the mentally handicapped from an holistic perspective and offered a movement experience that recognised their challenge in understanding their body, in developing relationships and in expressing themselves in some manner. Gallahue (1989) strongly supports the interrelated nature of development referring to the work of Bloom who began the development of a taxonomy of educational objectives - the cognitive, affective and motor domains (Bloom 1956). He believes it unfortunate that many see each domain as an 'independent entity of human development and learning' (p. 16). We can argue that the needs of the mentally handicapped are only different in degree from the needs of all members of society. Because SDM does interrelate the three domains of Bloom and is based on such sound movement principles it has been shown to be adaptable in addressing the needs of individuals and populations in a variety of contexts.

The approach that Sherborne brought to her teaching, perhaps intuitively or by design or indeed a recognition of both, was from a humanistic perspective. She acknowledged the holistic nature of each individual even within the framework of a group approach. In addition she explored the potential of how people with differing strengths and weaknesses could work together to create a mutually enriching experience. As referred to earlier in the chapter this has strong similarities with the philosophical base of James McMillan and the Halliwick swimming method. I quoted from an article by Joan Martyn (1981) on "The Halliwick Method" that the swimmer/instructor pair becomes a unit within a group activity' (p.288) and is a mutually enriching experience. Halliwick's work based on his experience as an engineer and on the hydrodynamic properties of water has, like SDM, been transferable to less disadvantaged groups than the physically handicapped. His work adds a new dimension to the teaching of swimming, not peripheral but with the potential to be central to the experience of both children and teachers.

I referred earlier to Conductive Education developed initially from the work of Professor Peto in Hungary. Again it places the individual at the centre of the experience. It recognises the weaknesses inherent in an approach where professional carers and therapists work largely independently with youngsters who have motor handicaps.

It is generally not appreciated how essential is the link between the different sections of life and the qualities of relations between people who live together is essential (Hary 1988).

Peto's work developed the idea of the conductor who organised all the relevant experiences for each individual.

The conductor exercises influence on the framework, on the whole and what is within it (Hary 1988).

This is not to attempt to compare Sherborne to a conductor nor to argue for her as a therapist but to acknowledge the similarities in approaches. Once acknowledged, the process of internalisation can begin and we see the strength to be gained in utilising the principles of her movement to enhance the learning process. Are these practitioners peripheral or with vision and understanding are they central to the developmental process of any individual ?

It is important for me to recognise that I am not a disciple - a slave to SDM. I am constantly looking for theoretically sound movement experiences to enhance the quality of life for the people with whom I work. In Physical Education, both in a mainstream and special context, I argue that I am reaching the majority of young people through current approaches to the physical curriculum. I admit to real delight to see the manner in which the teaching of games has adapted to new generations of learners; to see gymnastic movement as one concept rather than, as in my training, Educational and Olympic; to see dance education placed firmly at the core of the curriculum and to see the importance given to the health and fitness of our youngsters through the research and practical application that has developed in this field. There has been change both in the movement material and in the approach to its delivery but my experience over the last 24 years in secondary, special and primary work still leads me to the notion that too many of our youngsters lack in movement confidence. I am fully aware of the simplistic nature of this statement given a lack of objective evidence. Indeed, will such evidence present itself in the assessment process under the National Curriculum? I feel there is a lack of adequate training for primary teachers and inadequate time allocation given to Physical Education as part of the overall school curriculum. Even if you subscribe only partially to my view of movement confidence I am sure that you could suggest many different reasons for such a position.

Given these observations how would I define movement confidence? Perhaps as a baseline in skills or as a performance in a particular activity? Or a combination of both? It is hard to quantify, but I argue that youngsters who seem comfortable with their movement can adapt this comfort into a variety of movement situations. Gallahue (1989) from a motoric perspective addresses the term adaptation in the debate over the developmental aspects of maturation and experience. He says that it is often used 'to refer to the complex interplay between forces within the individual and the environment' (p. 15).

Berk (1991) from the psychological perspective returns to Piagetian theory for her understanding of adaptation. She feels that it is a process in which 'mental structures achieve a better fit with external reality through the complementary processes of assimilation and accommodation (p. 1). Sherborne (1990), in a summary of her movement form, lists several areas of the physical curriculum - apparatus, swimming, sports, dance - and believes that such activities are approached with more confidence if children have achieved 'some degree of body mastery and have learned to adapt and relate to other people' (p.111).

It is clear that the notion of adaptation is both significant and challenging in this view of movement confidence and Sherborne again helps me to make sense of this complexity from the experiential viewpoint when she says 'Developmental movement can provide a basis from which children can explore other activities (p.111). I argue strongly that movement confidence should not be peripheral but should be recognised as central to the overall development of any individual. SDM is not the answer to helping to achieve this goal but it is part of the answer. I see five key objectives to enhance growth in movement confidence:

1. to develop trust between youngsters;
2. to enhance the understanding of their body;
3. to allow them to experience a range of bodily actions in a non judgmental manner;
4. to reinforce notions of personal and general space through movement experiences that are inherently enjoyable; and
5. to introduce young people to Laban's effort qualities through a similar environment.

Movement confidence can lead to skilled performance which in turn enhances self-esteem and feeds itself with a motivation to learn in other areas. As in any developmental process we move from the simple to the complex in gaining control of our environment. SDM has been peripheral in this process. However, it was recognised by the Physical Education Working Party (1991) in their report to the National Curriculum Council, in the context of special children.

> Some children obtain great benefit from particular systems of movement education such as the Sherborne method which helps them develop confidence not only in their own bodies but also in trusting others (p. 36).

Sadly it was dropped as the documentation evolved! Nevertheless, I do believe that if we have the confidence to draw Sherborne into the centre of teaching and learning then we are taking a step along an exciting road. If movement is acknowledged as such a significant part of the developmental process then a movement form which enables us to enhance movement confidence can surely make a major contribution to the total educational experience of all our youngsters. It may not be as a causal link in this debate. However, I believe it does have something though it may have been ahead of its time. It may still be peripheral and it will take more than belief to establish a greater centrality but I hope that this chapter has been a contribution in the journey towards that goal.

References

Berk, L (1991)Child Development 2nd Edition Allyn and Bacon

Button, L (1976) Developmental Group Work with Adolescents Hodder and Stoughton

Clement, A (1994) The Teaching of Physical Skills Betty Hartman Brown and Benchmark

DES (1991) Physical Education Working Party: Physical Education for ages 5-16

Gallahue, D (1989) Understanding Motor Development

Hary, M (1988) The Human Principle in Conductive Education International Institute, Budapest

Keogh, J and Sugden, D (1990) Problems in Movement Skill Development University of South Carolina

Martyn, J (1981) The Halliwick Method Physiotherapy October Vol 67, 10

Orlick, T (1978) The Co-operative Sports and Games Book Pantheon

SCAA (May 1994) Physical Education in the National Curriculum draft proposals (School Curriculum and Assessment Authority)

SCAA (1994) The National Curriculum and its Assessment (Final Report) Sir Ron Dearing (School Curriculum and Assessment Authority)

Sherborne, V (1990) Developmental Movement for Children Cambridge: CUP

Warnock, M (1978) Special Educational Needs HMSO

Williams, A (1989) Issues in Physical Education for the Primary Years Falmer

Yardley, A (1972) Movement and Mental Activity Child Education May

Chapter 3

The Essence of Sherborne's Work:
The Way Forward

Maureen Douglas

Inevitably each of us will have a personal perception and understanding of Sherborne Developmental Movement (SDM) work; a perception most probably coloured by our first meeting with her work and drawn from our extended experience of it. It seems that often innovative movement practitioners, which I believe Veronica was, have been charismatic teachers. (Laban and Feldenkrais may be examples to place alongside Sherborne). People such as these can impact on those they teach and there is a consequent danger of a legacy which is subjective. It is therefore important to take an empirical historical approach and examine the evidence available in order to arrive at some understanding of the person and her work in the context of her time.

To gain some sense of the 'essence' of Veronica Sherborne's work two questions will be considered: What are the critical features of the work and what is unique about it? My three main sources of evidence to investigate are text, videotape and personal recollection.

Of text it can be said that there was little published by Veronica who finally said in 1990, "Now the time has come for me to write about my work myself". The few conference papers published have proved worthy of study and they show the development of her thinking evolving through her experience. The 1965 address to a Movement Therapy conference is particularly interesting in this context. It is also encouraging that there is evolving a body of text about her work to which these conference proceedings may contribute.

The video material produced by Sherborne suggests a diversity of application for this work. It includes work with mentally handicapped children (A Sense of Movement 1976), with mainstream children (A Matter of Confidence 1970), with the integration of handicapped children into mainstream work (Good Companions 1985) and work with mentally handicapped adults (Building Bridges 1982). So we have evidence of a diversity of application for SDM and the multidisciplinary gathering at the conference was a healthy continuation of that.

The third source, personal evidence, will have particular limits and it may be problematic in some ways, but it must become valued evidence. We must analyse what we have learnt from being taught and from seeing developmental movement in practice.

I want first to reflect on two characteristics of Sherborne as a teacher. I refer to her exploration of the phenomena of movement and her concern for the process of the session with children. My personal awareness of this derives from limited experience of her teaching when she contributed to a conference on Physical Education for children with Special Educational Needs at Rolle[1] in 1986. As she taught and spoke there was a real sense of her continued thoughtful engagement with the movement experience and the teaching process. The model of the reflective practitioner is much talked about in education in UK today, and it is indicated in the 1985 address on Movement and Youth when she acknowledges and owns the processes of trial and error, critical self assessment, continued experiment and learning from experience. She attended to both movement content and teaching.

---

[1] Rolle Faculty of Arts and Education, The University of Plymouth.

I suggest that the continuing fascination with and exploration of movement is the tradition of movement practitioners and thinkers of the nineteenth and early twentieth century. By placing Sherborne in a time context and considering a continuum of thought we may learn how she gains from, and adds to earlier work.

I refer to Delsarte (1811-1871) whose quest was to understand the process of expression through the arts. He focussed on movement and concluded that the phenomena could reflect our personal feelings and so through the arts could be expressive of them. This led Delsarte to extend his observation and to formulate an analysis of human gesture. His intention that this should become a tool for actors may not have been recognised but his clear statement of relationship between emotion (feeling) and movement did influence others. I also pause to note that it is said that he was still learning about movement, he like Sherborne was continually observing and exploring movement.

More recently but in the same tradition there is evidence of Laban's lifelong dynamic involvement with movement (1888-1958). Listening to those who worked with him one gained a sense of his lifelong fascination with movement. His writings show the development of thought, from his early experience of being moved by natural beauty and finding dance the only way to express his feeling, through his extended analysis of movement to the breadth of his more philosophic musing (Thornton 1971, Hodgson & Dunlop 1990). The varied facets of his thinking are reflected in many of the papers published by the Laban Guild and his continued engagement with movement experience is indicated in Lisa Ullman's (1960) preface to the second edition of the History of Movement when she states that at the time of his death Laban was planning a revision of his original text.

It is interesting to contextualise Sherborne by reference to these two somatic thinkers. Their work must be set against nineteenth century dualist thought but both hold a more holistic concept of the individual. Laban used the term 'body-mind' to try to capture the wholeness of the person. This extensive work on effort, the dynamic quality of movement and its relationship to feeling and emotion began, like Delsarte, in his work as a artist and dancer but led him to work in education and therapy. Through his experiences with movement choirs, dance forms and his work with Lawrence in industry, Laban's recognition of the affective power of movement for the individual was strengthened.

From this reflection I draw two points. Firstly, that as with Delsarte and Laban the exploration of movement is important for us as practitioners. Continued movement experience and consideration of how that experience affects us is essential to our understanding and I believe it is critical that our knowledge must be body knowledge if we are to be effective in our handling of movement sessions for teaching. Secondly, I suggest that Sherborne is part of a continuum involved in shifting the focus of movement practice from the arts to education and to therapy. This shift is reflected in her personal development having begun in education and become involved with dance within education, she became concerned with the therapeutic use of dance and movement, working with mentally and physically handicapped individuals. She allowed her work and herself to change and we must allow our work to change and shift, if it is to remain dynamic.

It is interesting here to consider parallels with the work of Dalcroze (1856-1950), an educationist concerned with improving learning, particularly in music, through using movement experience. He evolved a system of movement experience to aid musical, specifically rhythmic, education. What has happened to this programme? It appears not to have had the same impact as Laban's work and seems to be very little known today. Why? It may be that geography is significant, Dalcroze worked in Europe and not in the United Kingdom and I suggest it is also because he appeared to have constructed a prescriptive set of exercises. Bachmaan in a 1991 text goes back to review the original work and suggests that there is, in fact, a set of experiences and the teacher must be creative within them.

14

What should we learn from this for the work of Sherborne? We need to look at her programme and her activities, to use them, to search for the principles underlying her work and to be creative within those principles. It is important to be dynamic in exploring the potential of the work and to prevent it becoming dead. Veronica's work is worthy of analysis and scrutiny but I suggest it will only survive if practitioners take the principles and develop within them, mindful that the power is in **the movement experience not the system.**

What are identified as the significant and critical features of the work?

1. Firstly, it is based on the recognition that movement has an affective power;
2. Secondly, the use of existing movement knowledge as a base for the continued personal exploration of the phenomena of movement is a characteristic of the practitioner; and
3. Thirdly, the attention to the importance of relationship as an experience and in delivering the movement work.

What is the evidence for stating that movement has an affective power? I have stated this as a belief of movement artists and it can reasonably be surmised that it was absorbed by Veronica in her Laban based training. It is in writing of her experience as a movement therapist working with clients who had severe emotional and psychological problems that she shows her ownership of that belief. I refer to her 1965 address on movement therapy which shows the seed of thought subsequently explored and incorporated into her teaching and writing. In this paper is an early suggestion of the statement that a child has two basic needs, of being comfortable in her body and of being able to relate to others. In the same paper she writes, "I do not think we know how important relationships to another person is". She poses the question, "How can we help cut off people communicate through movement?" identifing touch and play as starting points. She also notes that partner work can be supportive and her paper clearly reflects Sherborne's experience of working with the affective power of movement.

We move on to consider that the use of existing movement knowledge is a base of continued personal exploration of movement. It has already been said that much was drawn from Laban's work and this is evidenced in the text of her book as well as the programme of activities. But, it is important to note that she took Laban's work and used it making her own sense of it. Consider the focus on body awareness; perhaps because of his origins as a dancer and choreographer, Laban was much concerned with the centred body in the context of the space, but Sherborne's focus is on the centre of the body as critical in knowing the self and giving confidence in the body.

Consideration of Laban's extensive work on 'effort' or movement quality leads me to ask a further question. Does Sherborne use a full and balanced range of dynamic quality? Consider the motion factor of weight, Laban identifies two aspects of experience, action and sensation - active movements include the push, punch or thrust, and I note the slow strong movements are used, are sudden strong movements also used? The sensation of heaviness occurs often at the end of a strong active movement and in moments of collapse, but when is the complementary quality of lightness used in Sherborne's work? When, in the action drive, are both fighting and indulging attitudes as defined by Laban represented? It may be for those involved in child therapy situations or psychotherapy work on lightness as a sensation is a long way from the present movement function of the client, but, for those using Sherborne work in mainstream education, there are many questions to ask about attention to effort and provision of a full and balanced range of experience.

Sherborne's attention to the importance of relationship has been mentioned in referring to her 1965 movement therapy paper. I suggest that her own work has evolved from Laban's analysis which included leading and being led, enfolding and being enfolded as significant relationship experiences. I consider that the clear identification of with, against, and shared relationship experienced through relationship play is a critical feature of the work.

Three significant features of Sherborne's work have been identified and it is important to place alongside these, an important principle of practice. The stress on the balance of the session must be noted. This may in part be traced back to Laban's work on rhythm and harmony, and his insistence of the importance of a balanced effort experience. Sherborne refers to the balance of 'quiet and more exciting activities within any one session and of the balance of giving and receiving movement experience, being active and passive in relationship ('Matter of Confidence' video sound track).

Having identified the essential features of the work, we come to a consideration of its uniqueness. I suggest this is a combination of developmentally appropriate movement experience and relationship play. When true play has a sense of joy we are fully engaged in our experience. This is both the power and the uniqueness of Sherborne's work as it contributes to personal development through being fully engaged in a movement relationship experience.

What are the ways forward for the Foundation? Collect more evidence of use - anecdotal evidence, collect more research based analytic evidence and extend the work to new directions. This can only be done if we absorb the work and 'live' it, having it as a way of practice. An example of this has been provided by Janet Sparkes (Chapter 15) who states that she could not think of any other way to work in Romania other than by using Sherborne work. We must also be aware of opportunities. Following an introduction to developmental movement for school counsellors, one of the participants observed that the work offered the potential to rehabilitate the abused child back into its body. Clearly the work could be used in varied fields.

In conclusion, I consider the way forward for us as individuals. I suggest three things;

i) keep moving and learning through new movement experiences;
ii) keep experimenting and trying things out; and
iii) keep playful, enjoy and engage with pleasure.

References

Bachmaan, M (1991) Dalcroze Today - an education through and into music Oxford

Feldenkrais, M (1972) Awareness Through Movement - health exercises for Personal Growth Harper Row

Hodgson, J & Dunlop, V P (1990) Rudolf Laban : an introduction to his work and influence Northcote

Laban, R (1959) in The Laban Art of Movement Guild magazine, Commemorative Issue.

Laban, R (1960) Ed Ullman Mastery of Movement 2nd Edition

Shawn (1974) (2nd Edition) Every Little Movement Dance Horizons NY

Sherborne, V (1965) paper presented to the Movement Therapy Conference, published in the Laban Art of Movement Guild magazine, May, 1966.

Sherborne, V (1970) A matter of confidence - work with mainstream children

Sherborne, V (1976) A sense of movement - work with mentally handicapped children

Sherborne, V (1982) Building Bridges - movement with mentally handicapped adults

Sherborne, V (1985) Good Companions - integration of special needs and mainstream children

Sherborne, V (1985) Movement for Children and Youth - keynote speech to the International Symposium on Adapted Physical Education - Toronto in Laban Guild Magazine Vol 75 1986

Sherborne, V (1990) Developmental Movement for Children CUP

Sparkes, J (1995) "Sherborne Movement in a Specific context" in J Dibbo and S Gerry (Eds) Physical Education. Therapy and Sherborne Developmental Movement Plymouth: University of Plymouth Press

Thornton (1971) A Movement Perspective of Rudolf Laban Methuen

Chapter 4

"I'm feeling good with you!"
Well-being and Sherborne Developmental Movement

Sue Gerry

Introduction

For many years I have been interested in alternative medicine and the commonly held view that it contributes towards a person's well-being. In fact at one stage in my career I trained as a homeopath to put my beliefs into practice. However, I feared treating people who were very sick in case I did not have the knowledge to make them well again! This influenced my decision to teach. Here I began the search for a way to encourage children to engage in physical activities both in school and after they had left the school gates which would contribute towards their sense of well-being. I have therefore, been able to integrate both my interests in health and Physical Education within my research. Over the years I have been working in schools with various 'hats' on ie; teacher, researcher, parent and governor, which has led me to recognise that the focus on health within primary schools has been more upon the fitness aspect of health rather than the development of total health. For example, teachers and those who teach teachers work on circuit training, aerobics and skipping exercises as a way to link fitness and health together. However, the continuing development of my own personal philosophies on holistic education has encouraged me to search for alternative ways to teach children about health within the framework of Physical Education. These ideas have been influenced by of the work of Veronica Sherborne and the learning theories of Vygotsky (1969), Applebee and Langer (1989), Hodgkin (1985), Watts and Bentley (1989) and Wood (1988). I argue that elements of these philosophies can be drawn together to create a framework where the child is treated from a monist rather than a dualist perspective. As such, I have begun to develop an alternative approach that I describe as Health Focused Physical Education (HFPE). This term, I feel has a wider application than the more popular terms of Health Related Exercise (HRE) and Health Related Fitness (HRF), which seem to concentrate predominantly on the physical dimension of our self.

In this paper I consider the necessary features of Health Guidance 5 (1990) which is a cross-curricular guidance document produced by the National Curriculum Council (NCC) for general curriculum planning and implementation in schools. I will specifically look at the notion of well-being as a requirement of this document. The three central issues I examine are the requirements of this NCC documentation, the concept of the whole child and the framework which Sherborne Developmental Movement (SDM) work offers to effectively manage the wider notion of health in Physical Education.

oOo

Within Physical Education health has been and still is on the political agenda; the emphasis seems to be on requiring Physical Education teachers to acknowledge the importance of health within their teaching programmes. With the HRE movement focusing on the physical aspect of the child, I suggest that the body is viewed instrumentally by concentrating mainly on the physical mechanisms. However, a wider perspective is emerging as Health Guidance 5 (1990) requires that health education's essential features are;

...the promotion of quality of life and the physical, social and mental well-being of the individual (p.1).

This has clear signals that to effectively teach HRE we need to consider a more holistic approach to Physical Education (Dibbo and Gerry 1995) which has a health focus. However, the model of health which the Health Guidance 5 document suggests recognises that exercise is a feature of promoting and maintaining good health and explicitly requires pupils to 'make positive choices about their own activities' (p.5) which, I argue, does not critically reflect on what is really meant by health, Physical Education and well-being.

So, implicit within the statements set out by the Health Guidance 5 (1990) document (p.1) are vast areas for discussion and analysis, for example; the notion of what is good health, the moral questions of what defines the quality of life, the social and cultural constraints on children in and out of school and the question of autonomy to mention a few. However, within the context of SDM teaching I will narrow my focus to examine the emotional and social dimensions of the child by looking at the concept of well-being and the quality of life. I have chosen these areas because underlying all Sherborne's philosophies are the ideas of the development of the psychological and social dimensions of the child. Nevertheless, in my search for an understanding of well-being, I do not seek to find the inaccessible single criterion or definition of the concept, but an attempt to understand what adults and children consider as their own sense of well-being in order to inform teaching in HFPE.

I believe that until we arrive at a common understanding of how our own sense of well-being is constructed within our everyday lives its promotion is problematic. The word 'well-being' is used as part of our everyday language but without a consensus of understanding for each individual. It is one of those aspects of our life which is taken for granted. Therefore, in practice it becomes necessary to search beyond the level of conversation where consensus is seen to exist to find out what health and well-being are really like and 'to bring into awareness what has been taken for granted' (Barritt, et al 1984 p.4). I attempt to discover how people construct these concepts to enable a greater understanding of the teacher teaching Physical Education and the childrens' feelings as they engage in Physical Education. Through the face to face situation of the teacher and child in the gym we can begin to make sense of the cultural lives, values and beliefs of our fellow human beings. I have approached this enquiry through existential phenomenology which offers a framework to question the world in which we live as human beings. The interpretive methodology exists to understand the following aspects of our lived experience:

1. **Temporality (lived time)** - this is not objective time but in thinking back to episodes in your life when you have enjoyed yourself, time *seems* to go faster and during periods of boredom the longer time *seems* to last - I will discuss this aspect through emotions and well-being, this will be in more depth than the following points because of its centrality to SDM;

2. **Spatiality (lived space)** - this is the space or environment in which we find ourselves and as such reflects how we feel. For example the gym or hall holds different meanings for us, some people relish the thought of being in a large open space ready to be active, others fear the idea because on previous occasions they have hurt themselves, been ridiculed by their peers or their teacher, or failed at a task. This space therefore affects how we relate to Physical Education and our fellow human beings - I will discuss this aspect briefly through relationships and well-being;

3. **Corporeality (lived body)** - as we live out our lives in and of our body, we experience different relationships to our own body, either that of an object when we think about brushing our hair or putting on our shoes, or as part of our very self in that we exist

always in a bodily world (van Manen, 1990 p.103). I will discuss this aspect briefly through physical appearance and well-being;

4. **Relationality (lived other)** - as we meet other people we develop a relationship to others and share interpersonal space, it is this aspect which gives us a communal sense to our life and perhaps contributes to the meaning of our life - I will discuss this aspect briefly through conditions for well-being.

Throughout I will use the context of the school, the classroom, the hall, the children and the teacher. Here we come face to face with each other and through experiences and discussion our existence becomes reality. In other words, we begin to make sense of ourselves as we move in an essentially social world where we engage in discourse and reflection. However, there may be inherent problems with taking people's views and opinions as a basis for data analysis in support of a particular hypothesis as only good common sense is relied upon. Nevertheless, this did not present a problem within this research as the aim has been to find out what sense people make of the world of health and Physical Education. As such, the data collected consists of written material from teachers and children, transcripts of the spoken word and written notes of observations. A generalisation of theory has not been the aim but rather the discovery of a commonality of themes of understanding. The goal of my analysis has been to examine the language that people use which captures central themes to the research or as some people call them, the structures which go to make up the analysis (Barritt et al, 1984 and Van Manen, 1990). Comparisons to the understanding of others through the written text act as a check on the reality of the intersubjective moment, thus contributing towards its validity.

Emotions and well-being - lived time

My initial questions were to discover how well-being is constructed in the everyday lives of adults and children, what do they consider as the most important contributors to their well-being? As such, I asked teachers, physiotherapists, psychologists, health educators, fitness experts and special needs teachers what this elusive term meant to them. Many found this a difficult question to answer at first, but after some thought they all responded that it was a 'feeling' of varying typifications. I have categorised them as follows;-

* aspects of the person eg; body image which included the notion of 'feeling fit' and 'feeling the right body weight';
* managing situations emotionally, cognitively and physically;
* being in a 'good' relationship; and
* having a sense of harmony or equilibrium in one's life.

From this information I gained clear signals that well-being is defined in many terms, however, a dominant feature of their responses was that of **emotional states**. Very often the term 'feeling good about myself' and 'feeling happy and content with myself' was used to describe this concept. From these initial findings I asked children what made them feel good as all the adults had responded that well-being was a positive dimension of their lives and the word 'well-being' I felt was too ambiguous for young children to understand. I asked the children what aspects of their life made them feel good. They identified 'happiness' as a feature of well-being, one child telling me that she felt "relaxed and in a better mood". Many of these words the children used were very nebulous and the children found it very hard to clarify their feelings further. This may be due to a number of factors; it may be that the children did not have the vocabulary to describe their feelings; or that children find it difficult to describe their emotional states unless they are clearly defined eg; anger or happiness. However, when I probed deeper with one child aged 8 about what she understood by the word 'good' she explained by saying that it was like "When there is a nice view in front and behind you". A description such as this animates our interests and we can begin to peek into the world of the child. Casey, (1987) and Smith (1992) consider that our body acts as a vessel of memory (p.71) which when we listen to children's descriptions or watch them engaged in some activity we are taken back to our own memories of participation in similar activities.

By listening to children's conversations about Physical Education we can begin to have an understanding of the physical experience not only through their experiences but through our own teaching and performance.

> ...what is best for this child, what can be better than attempting to define this present activity as the stuff of good memories. Such a procedure I believe stands a good chance of 'respecting the child's experience', of 'thinking it positively', and thus of seeing it's pedagogic experience (Smith, 1992 p.73).

This careful listening enables us to hear what the child is really saying. Yet, if those very same children describe some aspects of their Physical Education lesson as giving them a sense of fear of failure, or fear of the space in which they move, then those conversations should be listened to by the educators. If well-being is not promoted through competitive sports and testing for fitness then we should think about alternative ways to approach the pedagogic experience. One approach may be through SDM where the children are able to experience an environment in which they can feel safe and secure, they can be valued and learn to work together in collaboration. The safe and secure environment created means that the children have emotional stability within what I argue can be a threatening learning environment unless handled in a sensitive way.

Relationships and well-being - lived relationship to other

The socially constructed world of humans beings enables us to attain shared meanings. Our notion of well-being therefore, is shared and constructed through our interaction with others. Many people I spoke to, whether children or adults, identified that relationships were an important contributor to their well-being. The following is a sample of the answers I received; - "Being in good relationships with important and close family members and friends is one aspect of well-being for me", "Feeling safe and secure in relationships", "My family, friends and colleagues being satisfied and appreciative of my efforts (whether successful or not!)", "Playing with my friends at home and school", "I'm happy when I can go round to play at my friend's house".

Through SDM the child is offered a caring and safe learning environment in which the child works closely with her friends, using her body to develop a "sense of wholeness" (Sherborne 1990 p.4). Sherborne's relationship work enables the child to understand not only their partner but themselves as well. Therefore, I am suggesting that through integrating SDM with HFPE well-being may be promoted.

Physical appearance and well-being - lived body

My interviews have also indicated that well-being is closely linked to the way people feel that they **should** look and the following extracts support this argument; "Well-being for me is liking how I look" and "When I feel the right body weight". Csikszentmihalyi (1992) supports this view when he states that;

> We most often associate our self with our body...the self is in many ways the most important element of consciousness, for it represents symbolically all of consciousness other contents as well as the pattern of their interrelations (p.34).

As such, the testing culture which is dominant within health and Physical Education may place the child in a threatening situation which affects her own sense of self and her own self image. If however, the child is enabled to experience a situation in which the emphasis moves away from fitness testing to a more holistic notion of health she can have more positive images of the body and therefore of her self.

Conditions for well-being - lived space

A definition for the quality of life has eluded clarification for centuries. Aristotle recognised this in his *Nichomachean Ethics* and said;

> ... when it comes to saying in what happiness consists, opinions differ, and the account given by the generality of mankind is not at all like that of the wise. The former take it to be something obvious and familiar, like pleasure or money or eminence and there are various other views, and often the same person actually changes his opinion. When he falls ill he says that it is health, and when he is hard up he says that it is money". Book 1. Chapter 4

The quality of life is socially constructed by us within our Western Liberal values and morals. Also we construct our notion of well-being from a universal value of what 'the good life' is. Perhaps there is a need to challenge this understanding and look more widely at what well-being is for the individual by exploring alternative ways to achieve this.

The child and well-being

> I have come to the conclusion that all children have two basic needs... they need to feel at home in their own bodies and so to gain body mastery (sic), and they need to be able to form relationships. The fulfilment of these needs - relating to oneself and to other people - can be achieved through good movement teaching (Sherborne 1990 p.v.).

Here, Sherborne accepts that movement is seminal to life, as did Laban (1960). Implicit within SDM is that if the child's sense of well-being is to be promoted then there is a need to consider the child as an interrelated whole and not just a body. Contributing towards the overall development of the child is achieved by recognising the importance of building positive relationships with and between children. Within the context of HFPE I am working towards a pedagogy which recognises explicitly that the child is more than a body to be exercised. This view has evolved from Sartre (1943) who identifies that if the body is viewed purely as an object we begin to view our own embodiment as that of a machine or mechanism. I suggest that this is the mode which the HRE and HRF movement has historically and currently directs their attentions. The body remains an object to be measured and categorised by looking at heart recovery rates, peak flow rates, desirable body weight, skinfold measurements etc. However, treating our body as an object (Merleau-Ponty, 1943 and Sartre,1948) is not the usual way in which we live out our lives, the natural mode is the 'body-for-self', classified as the lived embodiment, our self being integral to our lived experience.[1]

Through, of and in our body we perceive the world and as such experience our existence. This is described as our embodied relationship and presents a monist perspective, seeing the individual intrinsically as an interrelated whole. SDM acts as a starting point for this philosophical debate in which we can be part of the world, aware of our body, yet still be in and of our body. Her work offers a safe, secure environment for the children by using "with" and "against" relationships. The movements begin close to the ground and gradually as the

---

[1] According to Husserl "The lifeworld which constitutes our lived experience, it simply is, the whole sphere of everyday experiences orientations, and actions through which individuals pursue their interests and affairs by manipulating objects, dealing with people, conceiving plans, and carrying them out". This life-world differs from one social group to the next, each group objectifying their spheres of experiences and unquestioningly accepting them as reality (Gurwitsch 1982 p.69).

children gain confidence they can initiate more risky movements at higher levels (Dibbo 1995 p.15). Essentially SDM involves building relationships; as the children and adults work together, they manage each others body weight, they manage their own body weight, they exercise responsibility and they are making decisions through talking, doing, reflecting and revisiting. The framework given also enables them to develop movement and body management skills.

Observing a session we see children working together, their bodies moving into various shapes and balances. Initially, to the onlooker we see the physical dimension of the children. However, by listening to conversations between the children as they work closely together, we realise that they are engaged in thinking about where they will put their bodies (corporeality), how they can trust and be trusted by their partners (relationality), how their body feels in the immediate space and that of the larger space of the hall (spatiality) and as they return to the classroom we hear them reflecting on what they have achieved and what the experience has meant for them (temporality). Thus, SDM involves the children in cognitive as well as physical skills and also acknowledges the importance of feelings (for the individual alone and for others). It concerns relationships and caring and for me, it meets the needs of the whole child in the Physical Education environment - the physical, the affective and the cognitive domains operating within a wider socio-cultural framework are integrated through SDM and HFPE.

The reality of the real situation

The philosophies underlying both SDM and the development of the National Curriculum documentation have a central theme of empowering the child with a sense of well-being. However, a feature of well-being is the emotional dimension yet, the Health Guidance 5 document does not explicitly acknowledge the emotional dimension of the child and the Educational Reform Act (1988) which set in place the National Curriculum states that the curriculum should be broad and balanced to 'promote(s) the spiritual, moral, cultural, mental and physical development of pupils at the school and of society'.

So, as my attention focused on the children and the teacher in the Physical Education setting I have sought to establish whether the emotional development of the child was an aim of education. Therefore, the intersubjective lifeworld of teachers, health educators and children was my focus as they defined the notion of well-being . In fact, one teacher I have interviewed does identify the development of an emotional sense of well-being for children as one of her goals for not only Physical Education but her total philosophy for education. The following transcript I feel captures these aspirations;

> Well, I think that I spend a huge percentage of my day really, trying to manipulate the activities so that it's a forgiving and generous environment. Not that it always is, but you have to try and I think that probably I put more energy in the day into that than the content of the work, because if the environment in which it happens isn't right then the content doesn't work so much... It's really part of the whole philosophy isn't it of airing comments and making it safe to say good things? 'Cos often we are shrinking violets and we don't know how to accept compliments that if you do it quite often then they think its alright to say, "Yeah I'm good at that", as long as you don't say it to the detriment of someone else, "I'm good at this and you're not"....(And) it's OK to make mistakes, one where the children can assess themselves and that they can say both positive and negative things about themselves.

> I sort of regard PE as a great friend in that it amplifies what I am doing elsewhere, but it does it in 30 minutes, whereas reading can take months for a child to realise that, and maths can be a term for a child who is not doing very

well. The child can go up into the hall and in twenty minutes can do something she couldn't do last week and then come down and she feeling good and then she can get out the maths books and she's still happy. So I find it has quite a knock on effect.

I think that it (building them up as a person) is my main aim in turning up for school everyday really. They've got to be numerate and literate in those particular skills but I want them to live with each other, but most of all I want them to be able to live with themselves, that's self esteem and recognising that I'm not good at this but I've got my own particular talents, they may not be the same as my best friend, but they are of equal worth. So that's where my energy seems to go.   (Primary school teacher).

However, the view of Physical Education being an integral part of the development of the whole child was not echoed by other teachers. In fact, the majority of teachers I questioned (7 out of 10) saw Physical Education as an arena for developing the physical skills of the child rather than for their overall holistic development.

To expect primary teachers, who do not have a specialism in Physical Education, to offer more than the development of a skills and techniques based HFPE curriculum may be too much. However, I would argue that many teachers already offer a model of good practise within the classroom which meets the needs of the whole child, but they do not always transfer their skills to the hall. Therefore, a method of teaching which enables teachers to transfer their skills from the classroom to the HFPE environment is, I feel, the way forward. Using some aspects of SDM as a framework for children to build relationships with the teacher and with each other, may act as a starting point before moving onto more risky areas of HFPE such as testing and weighing. This framework has for me some of the answers to those dilemmas which I have outlined.

Conclusion

To develop a sense of well-being in Physical Education lessons, using SDM, children need to explore more than just the development of skills and techniques; teachers can encourage the development of trust, collaboration and differentiated tasks which can contribute to the childrens' sense of well-being. At its simplest, the notion of well-being may be described as feeling good about oneself, not in isolation from others but in collaboration with others - it is the notion of independence yet interdependence. As J-P Sartre said we can never be free from, but we can be free for. I take this to mean free to define and redefine my self, free to make life choices and free to acknowledge that I live in conjunction with others working towards a sense of collaboration and well-being.

References

Applebee, A (1989) "The Enterprise we are part of: Learning to Teach" in P Murphy and B Moon (Eds) Developments in Learning and Assessment Open University Press: Hodder and Stoughton.

Aristotle Nichomachean Ethics Book 1

Barritt, L Beckman, A J Bleeker, H (1984) "Analysing Phenomenological Descriptions", Phenomenology and Pedagogy Vol. 2 No. 1

Casey, E S (1987) Remembering: A Phenomenological Study Bloomington, IN, Indiana University Press

Csikszentmihalyi, Mihaly (1992) Flow - The Psychology of Happiness Harper and Row, USA

Department of Education and Science (1988) Educational Reform Act London: HMSO

Department of Education and Science (1990) Physical Education in the National Curriculum London: HMSO

Dibbo, J (1995) "Doing and Talking, Approaching Gymnastics Through Sherborne Teaching Methods" in J Dibbo and S Gerry (Eds) Physical Education, Therapy and Sherborne Developmental Movement Plymouth: University of Plymouth Press

Dibbo, J and Gerry, S (In press Spring 1995) "Physical Education Meeting the Needs of the Whole Child" in British Journal of Physical Education

Griffiths, Morwenna (1993) "Education Change and the Self" in British Journal of Educational Studies Vol 41.2, June 1993 pp150-163)

Gurwitsch, A (1982) "Husserl's Theory of the Intentionality of Consciousness" in H L Dreyfus (Ed) Husserl, Intentionality and Cognitive Science

Hodgkin, R A (1985) Playing and Exploring Methuen, London and New York

Laban, R (1960) (Ed) Ullman Mastery of Movement 2nd Edition

Merleau-Ponty, M (1942) The Structure of Behaviour Methuen (1965)

Sartre, J-P (1943) Being and Nothingness Methuen University Paperback (1969)

Sherborne, V (1990) Developmental Movement for Children Cambridge: Cambridge University Press

Smith, S J (1992) "Studying the Lifeworld of Physical Education: A Phenomenological Orientation" in A Sparkes (Ed) Research in Physical Education and Sport: Exploring Alternative Visions London: Falmer Press

Van Manen, M (1990) Researching Lived Experience The Althouse Press, University of Western Ontario, Canada

Vygotsky, L S (1987) Thought and Language Newly revised and edited: MIT Press, Cambridge, Massachusetts

Watts, D and Bentley, M (1989) "Constructivism in the classroom: Enabling Conceptual change by Words and Deeds" in P Murphy and B Moon (Eds) Developments in Learning and Assessment The OU Press: Hodder and Stoughton

Wood, D (1988) How Children Think and Learn London: Falmer Press

Chapter 5

Doing and Talking:
Approaching Gymnastics Through Sherborne Teaching Methods

John Dibbo

Taking a reflexive approach to teaching has led me increasingly to a critical engagement with my own personal history as a student and teacher. As I teach and conduct research in Physical Education I continually question what I do! From an underlying holistic philosophy I feel that as I teach I should try to meet the needs of the whole child in the Physical Education lesson. There are many strategies that can be adopted to achieve this aim, however, the focus here is to explore the potential within Sherborne Developmental Movement (SDM) to meet this goal. I believe that using the ideas of Veronica Sherborne in my teaching has provided me with some answers to the questions I have raised. Indeed, it is these questions, and some of the answers I have found, that I would like to discuss in this paper.

My views about teaching and learning were influenced in the early 1970's by theories prevalent at the time I was trained to teach Physical Education, drawing significantly on Piaget's cognitive theory which portrayed the learner as active, trying to understand his environment, using prior knowledge and moving through the processes of assimilation and accommodation. As the teacher I was seen as an enabler who facilitated learning by providing appropriate learning opportunities, someone who gave the children the opportunity to try gymnastics, to experiment with moves on the floor and apparatus and to create movement sequences in this environment. Once the children had created these movement patterns I would then comment on and suggest ways to improve their work. This is a simple description of what was called "Educational Gymnastics" (Bilborough and Jones 1963). In contrast, as a student of Physical Education I was coached in Olympic Gymnastics. This created a dilemma for me, as on the one hand I was coached directly on my own performance but on the other hand as a teacher, I was taught to create appropriate learning environments for the children where the idea of 'instruction' and learning was somewhat limited. Learning was constrained by the notion of 'readiness to learn'(Piaget)[1] and no amount of instruction would influence this rate of progress.

However, subsequent studies, research and indeed, my own teaching since the early 1970's have made clear to me that whilst children may go through stages of learning their progress can be significantly influenced by appropriate instruction. Hodgkin, (1976 pp 73-78 on instruction and 1985 p. 92 on learning and instruction p. 93) as he develops a definition of instruction in his discussion of the 'teacher's roles in relation to the process of discovery' (1985 p. 91), creates a sound argument that reflects my thinking about and experience of teaching beyond my initial teacher training.

> Instruction involves bringing the learner confidently up to his frontier so that
> he begins to ask interesting questions, finds some answers, creates appropriate
> models or pictures and, perhaps, does some experiments. Such activity will
> only be appropriate and interesting if there is a hidden structure on which the
> learner's probe can touch (p. 93).

This interpretation of instruction by Hodgkin introduces for me 5 issues central to teaching and

---

[1] His basic idea was that children pass through stages of development and he argued that children cannot learn or be taught to function at higher levels before they have passed through the lower levels. This formed the basis of his notion of 'readiness to learn'. Wood 1988 page 7.

learning when he writes about:

    i)   'bringing the learner',
    ii)   'to ask .. questions',
    iii)   'creates appropriate models',
    iv)   'does some experiments' and
    v)   'a hidden structure'.

All these issues I locate within what has come to be known as social constructivism. Briefly, some assumptions about social constructivism include:

    i)   Firstly, children play an active role in learning;
    ii)   Secondly, as active problem-solvers children construct representations of experience in the mind;
    iii) Finally, language and communication play a fundamental role in the learning process as does the sharing of understanding and collaboration with adults and peers.

These I see located within a particular historical and socio-cultural framework which the children bring to the learning situation to be defined and redefined (Dibbo and Gerry 1995).

So, with these issues in mind, in my teaching of Physical Education I determined to move away from just the physical and to value the child more holistically (within a monist framework[2]) so that they are enabled to understand the whole (learning) experience for themselves. For me a social constructivist framework enables me to be more aware of how I can help the child make sense of the learning experience in Physical Education. Therefore, I see my role as the...

teacher (who) helps by constructing meaningful activities... and...structures the learning experience so the children have appropriate strategies to work successfully (Dibbo & Gerry 1995).

I believe that the old idea that the child learns when he is 'ready' and that teachers diagnose what the child knows and then fill in the missing pieces disenfranchises the child in the learning process. Though direct teaching, for example, may have a place in gymnastics teaching in response to learning basic moves and dealing with basic errors, a contingent teaching style (which I explain below) more thoroughly involves the child in the process of learning. In the direct style the teacher identifies the weakness, suggests ways forward and monitors the childs' performance offering corrections as appropriate. However, it is not simply my intention to reject this and other more scientifically determined styles of teaching (Mosston and Ashworth 1989) but to draw on the more holistic theories of learning and consider the notion of social constructivism. In this framework the teacher can be described as a "contingent teacher" operating within a social constructivist framework who:

...helps children construct local expertise - expertise connected with that particular task ... by focussing their attention on relevant and timely aspects of that task (Wood 1988 p. 80).

---

2 Monism refers to the body lived holistically and pre-reflectively as the self (Horton-Fraleigh 1987). The body can exist as an object when reflecting on the known (ie the physical body) but can only be 'lived' when considered as an interactive, interrelated wholeness. Therefore, the notion of monism suggests that through education the body should not be treated from the perspective of an object but needs to be considered more holistically; the body and mind being one construct inseparable from each other. Without our body we do not exist, from this we assemble our socially constructed self, a point of centrality to our embodied beings (Whitehead 1987). [Definition developed by Gerry 1993, unpublished PhD research]

This also places the child at the centre of the learning experience and is where the teacher needs to provide the children with the skills to do the job [enabling skills]. Thus, with the teacher providing appropriate support learners are able to engage in new and more difficult tasks;

> By helping the child to structure his activities, we are helping him perform things he could not do alone until such time as he becomes familiar enough with the demands of the task at hand to develop local expertise and to try things for himself (Wood 1988 p.77).

I believe that for children to learn effectively in gymnastics, being taught within a social constructivist framework, they need:

i) to know how to move;
ii) to have the words to think, describe, communicate, and share their experiences;
iii) to have confidence in themselves and others as gymnasts;
iv) to be able to order and manage their actions and thoughts, to interpret what they have seen, to respond to the task set;
v) to be able to observe and comment on movement;
vi) to give appropriate feedback.

[Currently I describe these as enabling skills]

For this to be successful the whole learning experience needs to be located within a non-threatening learning environment. SDM[3], I argue, offers an excellent approach to teaching and learning that enables the children to develop the necessary confidence and movement vocabulary in a safe and non-threatening environment. However, when we take social constructivism into the classroom and the gym we also need to be aware of the nature and implications of the environment for the children in our care. For example, research into science education by Mike Watts and Di Bentley (1989) led them to develop this notion of a non-threatening learning environment from their research in which they found:

> on the whole, life in classrooms is conducted in a fairly robust atmosphere, redolent of the normal chiding, teasing and banter that occurs within pupil peer-group and teacher -pupil interactions. On the heavy-handed side, sarcasm, abrasive wit and verbal bullying are not uncommon tools in the armoury of the hard pressed teacher - or youngster (p.160).

---

[3] **What does Sherborne work do for the gymnast and the teacher?**
It is safe and secure, using 'with' and 'against' relationships which are close to the ground then moving on to more risky levels. It involves relationships as children and people work together, they manage each others body weight, they manage their own body weight, they exercise responsibility and they are making decisions. They are given a movement framework from which they can develop movement skills and body management skills. It is physical but also cognitive and acknowledges the importance of feelings (for the individual alone and for others), relationships and caring. I suggest that is meets the needs of the whole child as the physical, cognitive and affective domains operate within a wider socio-cultural framework and are integrated through a Sherborne approach to gymnastics.

For the gymnast it explores strength and stability, it explores tension and relaxation, it gives confidence in self and others, it inspires trust, it explores partnership work, it provides a framework for quality and working in this way seems to give the children pleasure, early success and confidence.

This description of the science lesson is not too far from that of the gymnastic lesson which also has the added pressure of the physical risk and the threat to the child's self esteem with the increased risk of public failure. Watts and Bentley (1989) describe the act of learning, in any environment, as an emotional affair where the affective and cognitive are not separate and distinct but are irrevocably intertwined. In gymnastics the physical has equal place as the learning experience brings with it the range of emotions 'from delight to fear, from satisfaction to frustration and despair' (p.161).

If I return to the interpretation of instruction from Hodgkin when teaching about stability using Sherborne's ideas the children are invited to make a stable base and then with their partner test the stability of this base. The teacher sets the task appropriately to the childrens' level of ability, the children discuss their work -'ask questions' and then share their ideas with others in the class (in groups of 4 or with the whole class) and through the use of language develop their cognitive understanding whilst working with and through relationships - a social constructivist framework which matches Hodgkin's idea of instruction. Such an activity is common place in gymnastics.

However, the careful structuring of the activity, elsewhere referred to as 'scaffolding' (Applebee 1989), provided for the children to help them carry out the task is critical. This is for me the 'hidden structure' described by Hodgkin. The task constructed in this way is not just physical, for example I encourage the children to do, think, reflect, talk and to revisit their work and ideas, all this is in a shared environment where relationships are crucial and where they need the 'skills' to do the job. It requires paired work (relationships) and it requires discussion (cognitive), it involves discovery and experimentation and it is owned by the children. This is to say that the outcome of the activity is not necessarily predetermined by the teacher (adult). It is the individual result of each child's (or group of children's) activities instead of a perfect but standardised forward roll, say, that is expected from a gymnast.

Teaching in this way requires, I believe, two essential prerequisites to ensure that effective learning takes place:

i)   the teacher must provide enabling skills for the children to manage the learning environment for themselves - the scaffolding described below;

ii)   the teacher must provide the appropriate level of support (teaching) at the right time - the contingent teacher.

In SDM, within a contingent teaching framework, the teacher tries to focus attention on the key elements of that activity to enable the child to manage the learning experience effectively. In a sense too, it is a means by which the teacher can structure the progression and continuity within the task for the child and ensure they reach a successful conclusion to the learning experience. Wood, Bruner and Ross (1976) introduce the metaphor 'scaffolding' to describe this aspect of the teaching process. Applebee (1989) defines the process more specifically as Instructional Scaffolding and identifies clearly a sequence to the process:

i)   Ownership - the child should make his own contribution to the task, open ended tasks, activities and problems;

ii)   Appropriateness -tasks should be too difficult for learner to complete on his own, but not so difficult that he cannot complete them with help. This implies careful staging of the activities we set/teach/match to ability and so on;

iii) Structure - sequence activities/skills/etc - but make them logical/accessible to the learner so he can use them independently;

iv) Collaboration - work with the learner - remove the elements of assessment and evaluation - ensure we do not test but teach!

v) Transfer of control - as the learner learns we can 'step back' and allow them to use the skills, knowledge and strategies we have taught and then give our attention to 'the next stage' of their learning. Within this framework the primary school teacher will set tasks or activities to complete or problems for the children to solve (p.221/222).

However, as a Physical Education teacher, I seek more from engagement in the task than the successful completion of a gymnastic performance, this is evident, I trust, from my comments so far. Within the social constructivist framework I see SDM teaching providing a context and method that enables the development of the physical yet, acknowledges the needs of the whole child leaving opportunity to meet the individual emotional, physical, intellectual and cultural needs of each child. The teacher creates a non-threatening learning environment, operates as a contingent teacher and within the teaching and learning framework the teacher tries to assess and meet the moment to moment needs of each child. This is an ideal which may not be achieved unless the teacher has provided, and continues to develop with the child, the enabling skills to meet these tasks and problems.

Conclusion

Veronica Sherborne's philosophy of teaching was significantly influenced by the teaching of Laban and then refined through considerable teaching experience, thought and discussion which I would describe as a reflexive approach to her work. The construct **reflexive** describes practice in teaching as where one is:

> able to perceive not only that one's personal history is influential in shaping one's world view, but also that this history is located in the midst of a larger socio-cultural canvas which too must be deliberated upon (Nias and Groundwater-Smith 1992 p. 93).

It is this particular **quality in the teacher** that I see as paramount in Sherborne's approach, which leads the search for good practice. For the learner SDM provides a sound basis for the development of body awareness, the development of self concept and self esteem in the individual, supports the development of the child and can contribute positively to the development of relationships in the growing child. For the teacher it locates the physical experience of Physical Education within an holistic framework by providing a range of movement activities that require thought and care. Thought in the sense that the child can interpret and develop the physical skills to their level of ability within a caring and safe environment. The caring and safe environment is also created through developing a sense of awareness for others by enabling children and adults to work together in partnership activities.

References

Applebee, A (1989) 'The Enterprise we are part of: Learning to Teach' in P Murphy and B Moon (Eds) Developments in Learning and Assessment Open University Press: Hodder and Stoughton.

Bilborough and Jones (1963) Physical Education in the Primary School University of London Press

Dibbo, J & Gerry, S (1995) "Physical Education: Meeting the Needs of the Whole Child" in The British Journal of Physical Education Spring Edition

Glasersfeld von E (1989) 'Learning as a Constructive Activity' in P Murphy and B Moon (Eds) Developments in Learning and Assessment Open University Press:Hodder and Stoughton.

Hodgkin, R A (1985) Playing and Exploring London and New York: Methuen

Horton-Fraleigh, S (1987) Dance and the Lived Body University of Pittsburgh Press.

Mosston, M and Ashworth, S (1986) Teaching Physical Education Merrill Publishing Company, 3rd Edition

Nias, J & Groundwater, S (Eds) (1992 The Enquiring Teacher Falmer

Watts, D and Bentley, M (1989) 'Constructivism in the Classroom: Enabling Conceptual Change by Words and Deeds' in P Murphy and B Moon (Eds) Developments in Learning and Assessment Hodder and Stoughton.

Whitehead, M (1987) A study of the views of Sartre and Merleau-Ponty and a consideration of these views for the justification and practise of Physical Education Unpublished PhD thesis.

Wood, D (1988) How Children Think and Learn Blackwell.

Wood, D J, Bruner, J S and Ross, G (1976) "The role of tutoring in problem solving" in Journal of Child Psychology and Psychiatry, 17, 2, pp. 89-100

Vygotsky, L (1962) Thought and Language USA, Massachusetts Institute of Technology.

Chapter 6

Developmental Movement as a tool to stimulate parent-child interaction in families with a handicapped youngster.

Gerrit Loots

The Context

As an early intervention team we started in 1982 to stimulate the development of the child with special needs during her first year of life. Because our approach was mainly directed towards the child we missed one of the most important components in the development of the child, the interactional context of the family. An overview of studies about the interactional context of young handicapped children shows the subtle way in which their development is influenced through parent-child interaction. Further, since researchers started to study language development in its social context conversational interchange has been recognised as a basic component of language learning.

In the case of a handicapped child an identifiable communication pattern that threatens the acquisition of linguistic skills can develop. Besides language learning the interactional context has an important influence on the socio-emotional development of the child. A disturbed interactional context can inhibit safe attachment and lead to problems in the child's further psychological development. Different studies stress the risk of disturbances in the case of children with special needs. As such, we introduced Sherborne Developmental Movement (SDM) in our intervention programme to establish whether this programme can improve the interactional context. These movement sessions were directed towards the members of the family of the child with special needs.

Introduction

The purpose of this paper is to present a way of using SDM in a context of early intervention. Because this approach is mainly based on practical and clinical experiences I think it is important to contextualise my work before starting. In 1982, the United Nations published their World Action Programme in which they stressed the importance of working with the families of disabled persons. It was in the same year that early intervention teams for families with disabled children were created in Belgium. Teams of medical specialists, psychologists, speech therapists, social workers and physiotherapists started to support families with disabled babies or toddlers in home-based programmes.

As a psychologist I was involved in a team of early intervention specialists working with sensory handicapped children. We had all been trained to direct our therapies towards the child's disabilities yet we were all convinced of a family centred approach. Nevertheless, for nearly five years we continued to work with traditional methods. At different times during the week home visits were arranged by speech therapists to train the child in auditory and language skills while the parents were watching and imitating the speech therapist or, even doing their housework. Other colleagues worked in a similar but uncoordinated way. In all cases the positive effects of this kind of early intervention were doubtful.

Is early intervention effective?

This was the title of a research report on the long term impact of early education for children from deprived homes or disadvantaged families (Bronfenbrenner 1974). Reviewing different studies Bronfenbrenner concluded that without family involvement intervention is unlikely to be successful and what few effects are achieved are likely to disappear once the intervention is discontinued. Clearly, the family seems to be the most effective for fostering and sustaining the child's development. The most effective period of family based intervention is during the first three years of life. Those strategies which focus attention on the interaction between parent and child around a common activity have been found to be critical. This approach is to be distinguished from the widespread traditional forms of parent education involving courses and counselling addressed only to the parent where there is no evidence to indicate the degree of effectiveness (Bronfenbrenner 1974).

These conclusions however, are based on studies concerning one specific population, i.e. the children of disadvantaged families. Therefore, care is needed in over-generalising these findings. Nevertheless, other authors working with other populations stress that the most effective intervention programmes are those focussing on the parent-child interaction (Anastasiow 1979).

Parent-child interaction

Since Winnicott (1957) identified that a woman during and especially towards the end of a pregnancy develops an increased sensitivity which enables her to adapt intuitively to her infant's need, an important amount of research on mother-child interaction has been published. Bowlby (1989) mentioned cycles of lively social interaction during the first weeks of life. Throughout these cycles the baby is likely to be as spontaneously active as his mother. The difference in their roles during this period is in the timing of their responses. Whereas an infants initiation and withdrawal from interaction tend to follow his own autonomous rhythm, the mother regulates her behaviour so that it meshes with that of her infant (Bowlby, 1989).

Papousek and Papousek (1983) ascribed a special role to visual behaviour describing it as a mechanism that helps selectively either to increase or reduce the amount of informational input. For every visual contact parents reward the newborn with a typical 'greeting response': retroflexion of the head, raised eyebrows and widely opened eyes. Collis and Schaffer (1975) noticed how mothers follow their baby's gaze in a room with brightly coloured toys. They established a mutual interest, commenting on the toy, naming it and manipulating it. A sharing experience is brought about, instigated by the infant's spontaneous attention to the environment but established by the mother who allows herself to be paced by the baby.

Kaye (1977) mentioned how mothers tend to interact during feeding in synchrony with the infant's pattern of sucking and pausing. During sucking the mother is generally quiet and inactive and during pauses she strokes and talks to her baby. Many more studies have been published and in all these a central theme of sensitivity is found. Parents seem to adapt themselves to the tune and rhythm of the infant, take his interests, signals and needs and feed them back in an expanding way, thus creating a dialogue.

According to Papousek and Papousek (1983) early interaction is based on two major factors with deep biological roots:

1 The newborn's integrative capacities; from birth a child is learning in a cross-modal way, integrating different experiences. This learning process occurs only under very favourable conditions.
2 The adults intuitive parenting; parental behaviour includes unconscious patterns of interaction creating this favourable condition.

Human infants are preprogrammed to develop in a socially cooperative way, whether they do so or not depends largely on how they are treated.

Characteristics of social interactions between mothers and their disabled infants.

Rogers (1988) in a review study examined the interaction during social play between mothers and their disabled children. For both she found the following social characteristics:

On behalf of the child:

1 Fewer and less readable cues;
2 Ignorance, avoidance and termination of social interactions;
3 Less positive-affect smiles, laughter and pleasant vocalisations;
4 More negative affect - frowns, crying, negative vocalisations;
5 Dampening of affect - less intense expression of affect;
6 Fewer turn-taking episodes;
7 More clashes;
8 Fewer initiations.

On behalf of the mother:

1. Higher level of control and initiations;
2. Less positive affect and pleasure;
3. Reducing reciprocity and synchrony
4. Specific adaptations; which can be positive (recalibration of affective levels by mothers of Down's syndrome infants); which can be negative (lack of pauses with premature infants).

In order to maximise the disabled child's social skills, it seems important to focus attention on characteristics of mother-infant interactions and to assist the two to develop maximally reciprocal, synchronised, enjoyable interaction patterns (Rogers 1988).

Using SDM in an early intervention programme for a family with a hearing-impaired youngster: an example.

The acquisition of language is one of the biggest problems in the education of hearing-impaired children of hearing families. In early intervention programmes most of the time is spent in the development of language. Since researchers started to study language development in its social context, conversational interchange has been recognised as a basic component of language learning. Indeed, conversational interchange is seen as both an important aspect of language development and the necessary condition of the development of other aspects of language; sounds, words, meanings and rule systems.[1] The way adults and young children interact seems to influence language acquisition. Studies about normal language development have shown typical features in the verbal interaction between mothers and their young children.[2]

From the start adults make their responses contingent upon the movements and interests of the infant (Collins and Schaffer, 1975). By acting in this way, they engage the infant in turn taking interactions and shared attentions which are the foundations of conversational interchange (Wood et al 1987). Early in the child's life, adults seem to accept the child as an

---

[1] For further work in this area please refer to De Paulo and Bonvillian 1978, Kaye 1977, Sachs and Johnson 1972, Schaffer et al 1977, Snow and Ferguson 1977, Stern 1974, Trevarthen 1979, Wells 1981 and Whitehurst et al 1972.

[2] For further work in this area please refer to Bonvillian et al 1979, Cross 1978, Ellis and Wells 1980, Furrow et al 1979, Moerk 1976, Sachs 1977, Snow 1977 and 1979 and Wells 1981.

equal conversational partner. They skilfully interpret the child's contributions, accepting their communicative intent. They adapt their own contributions to help the child to understand what is meant and to use the language as a model from which to construct their own linguistic knowledge. They tend to fit in their talk with the child's linguistic abilities facilitating the language learning task of the child.[3]

The interactional context of young hearing-impaired children

An overview of research about the interactional context of young hearing-impaired children indicate a typical communication pattern.

AUTHOR	SUBJECT	AGES	METHODOLOGY
Brinch, PM (1980)	Verbal and nonverbal mother-child interaction	5-6 years	Comparative study matched for age with hearing group

RESULTS
- mothers of deaf children used more attention-related behaviours; more questions and instructions.
- deaf children used more attention-related behaviours; less questions and instructions.

AUTHOR	SUBJECT	AGES	METHODOLOGY
Cheskin, A (1981)	Verbal mother-child interaction	1.6 - 2.10 y	Descriptive study about language structure and content

RESULTS
- mothers used short grammatically complete sentences; repetitions and restrictive vocabularies; frequent repetitions of own utterances; a high incidence of verbal labels.
- Mothers quickly supplied correct answers to their own questions

AUTHOR	SUBJECT	AGES	METHODOLOGY
Cheskin, A (1982)	Verbal mother-child interaction	1.6 - 2.10 y	Descriptive study about language function

RESULTS
- mothers used speech most frequently to control their children's behaviour and to describe objects and actions.

AUTHOR	SUBJECT	AGES	METHODOLOGY
Hughes, M E (1983)	Verbal mother-child interaction	3.4 - 5.6 years	Comparative study matched for language level with hearing group

RESULTS
- The verbal interaction between mothers and hearing-impaired children is very much like that between mothers and normally hearing children of similar

---

[3] For further work in this area please refer to Beckwith 1977, Cross,1977, De Paulo and Bonvillian 1978, Drach 1969, Holzman 1974, Moerk 1976, Newport 1977, Phillips 1970 and 1973, Remick 1976, Schaffer 1977, Snow 1972, 1976 and 1977 and Wells 1981.

36

linguistic levels.
- Mothers of hearing-impaired children repeated themselves more and used more naming; fewer questions; more declaratives (=older style)

AUTHOR	SUBJECT	AGES	METHODOLOGY
Nienhuys,T G, Cross, T G and Horsborough, (1984)	Verbal mother-child inter- action	2 and 5 years	Comparative study matched for - age - ability with hearing group

RESULTS
- Differences in maternal speech to age matched hearing and deaf children tend to ameliorate when child groups were matched for language ability (= most powerful determinant of maternal speech adjustment).
- Deafness characterises maternal speech: speech complexity remains on a level of prelingual hearing infants. No increase according to the child's development; reduced disfluency and more acceptability; more formal conversations. Mothers tend to be "language-models"; more run-on utterances; tendency to monologic interactions and lower conversational expectations less maternal expansions; higher use of self repetitions.

AUTHOR	SUBJECT	AGES	METHODOLOGY
Lyon, M (1985)	Verbal mother-child inter- action	pre-school age	Longitudinal study (12 months) to look at the effects of discourse strategies of mothers on the language development of hearing-impaired children

RESULTS
- Greater maternal control of the interaction is negatively associated with language improvement: utterances to direct; mother-initiated-bouts; mother's total contributions to the talk; maternal-repeat-utterance.
- The more active the child's role in the conversation the more the language improved: child's total contributions to the talk; child using questions; child-repeat-utterances; child-initiated-bouts;
- The more the two talked to each other reciprocally the more language improved: total number of utterances use of complex bouts instead of simple bouts, maternal use of genuinely information seeking questions.
- Those feature positively associated with language improvement were positively associated with age and negatively associated with hearing-loss.

AUTHOR	SUBJECT	AGES	METHODOLOGY
Chadderton, JH, Tucker, IG and Hostler (1985)	Verbal and non-verbal mother- child interaction	6 -36 months	Descriptive study about assessing the responsiveness of M mothers to their child's communica- tive initiations

RESULTS
- All the mothers were highly responsive to their child's initiating moves.
- The children expect an appropriate response to their initiating moves.
- The child's lack of ability or willingness to re-initiate seems to have an effect on language development.

These results are consistent with the earlier literature concerning the interaction between mothers and their young hearing impaired child.[4] Also, all these results seem to reveal an underlying communication mechanism. When adults find it difficult to establish reciprocal communication with a child, they may adapt by emphasising more control in the conversational interchange or discourse; they take a more active role in order to keep the dialogue ongoing and the child reciprocally takes on a more passive role and gets excluded from the acquisition of linguistic skills. We can find the same communication mechanism within the results of studies concerning the interaction of mothers and their mentally retarded children (Kogan et al 1969, Marshal et al 1973 and Cunningham et al 1981) or within the results of studies concerning the interaction between mothers and their language disordered children (Conti-Ramsden and Friel-Patti 1984, Davis et al 1988, Gardner 19889 and Schodorf and Edwards 1983). Therefore, to break through the establishment of this communication mechanism, we introduced SDM to our early interventions.

Sherborne's Developmental Movement Programme

Veronica Sherborne studied Physical Education and physiotherapy in the 1940's. She specialised in the methods of Rudolf Laban, a choreographer, who created the Art of Movement Studio in Manchester to study dance and movement. She used Laban's movement observations and analysis when she was involved in movement education with severely retarded children. Through trial and error she slowly developed her own movement programme for severely retarded children. She realised that the exceptional child has two basic requirements before he can learn and develop. These are body awareness or self-awareness and awareness of others, or the capacity to make relationships (Sherborne 1985 and 1989). She stated that you cannot learn about the world unless you have a starting place; an identity, and you cannot learn from other people unless you can relate to them (Sherborne 1985). In her book Developmental Movement for Children (1990) she stated:

> Through my experience of teaching and observing human movement, and of learning through trial and error, I have come to the conclusion that all children have two basic needs: they need to feel at home in their own bodies and to gain body mastery, and they need to be able to form relationships. The fulfilment of these needs-relating to oneself and to other people can be achieved through good movement teaching (p. v).

Body awareness and awareness of others are the two most important aims of SDM. Here I will only focus on the awareness of others or relationship play.

Relationship play

Sherborne distinguished in her work three kinds of relationships:

1. "With" relationships involve partners in caring, containing and supporting activities. The adult supports the child to experience joyful movements; he has to adjust to the needs and feelings of the child and when the child gives his weight, he is gaining confidence in the adult. When the child begins to respond to the movement play and

---

4 For further work in this area please refer to Altshuler 1974, Cross, Nienhuys and Morris 1980, Evans 1975, Goss 1970, Greenstein 1975, Gergory 1976, Gregory, Mogford and Bishop 1979, Kretchmer and Kretchmer 1979, Ling and Ling 1978, Myklebust 1964, Meadow et al 1981, Schlessinger and Meadow 1972, Simons-Martin 1978 and Vernon 1972

initiates new ways of playing, the adult imitates the child's initiations and feeds it back to the child. Through these careful sensitive reactions of the adult, the child gains self-confidence. A two-way play or reciprocal play can begin. Partners can reverse roles so that the child can learn to look after and be responsible for another person, even an adult.

Some activities:
Containing and supporting
The adult sits behind the child and makes a 'house' using arms, legs and trunk to contain the child. The adult cradles the child and takes his weight as they sway from side to side (Sherborne 1989).

Rocking horses
Cradling from side to side can be changed to rocking backwards and forwards. The adult sits with the child between his legs, both facing forwards and grasps the child under the knees. The adult then tips back and then forward. As the child feels safe, the adult tips so far back that the child is upside down with his feet in the air (Sherborne 1990).

Aeroplanes
The adult lies face up with legs bent up supporting the child's stomach and legs along the shins and holding the child on the shoulders. The child is above the adult, facing down in a flying position. The adult moves his legs gently forwards and backwards (Sherborne 1990).

Rolling
The adults sits with the child lying across his thighs and can then roll the child down to his ankles, up to the adult's nose and back to the thighs again.

2. **"Against"** relationships involves activities such as pushing over, testing a curled up parcel or testing each other's ability to stick to the floor. In all these activities the aim is to build up the child's strength, stability and to develop self-esteem. The child also concentrates on his own body energy. He has to unite and direct all his strength which requires focused attention and concentration. Last but not least, the child is stimulated to test the strength and stability of his partner. As opposed to winning, the child learns to control and adjust his own strength to the strength of his partner. He learns to be sensitive.

Some activities:
Squashing
The adult lies on top of and across the body of the child on the floor. The child is encouraged to wriggle out from underneath the adult's body. The adult only rests as much weight on the child as the child can cope with and the child experiences great satisfaction and a sense of achievement on escaping (Sherborne 1990).

Rocks
The child sits with knees bent up and feet apart and "sticks" to the floor using hands and feet. The adult tests this "rock" by pushing gently on the knees and then the back, strengthening the child's ability to be stable and strong (Sherborne 1989).

Back to back
The adult and child sit back to back, knees bent up. They plant their feet into the ground in a firm, wide base in front of them and their hands press into the floor behind them. They then push backwards against each other and see how strong their partner is, resulting in a static battle.

3. **"Shared"** relationships are symmetric relationships. They require simultaneous mutual dependence and mutual support. This is seen when partners sit facing each other and make a see-saw. Partners have to listen to their own bodies and to their partner's bodies at the same time. In shared relationships the adult and the child learn to cooperate as equal partners.

Some activities:
See-sawing
The adult and child sit facing each other grasping wrists. They take turns lying back and sitting up, and particular notice is taken as to whether heads are resting on the floor when lying back, and the child helps to pull the adult up into sitting (Sherborne 1989).

Balancing
The adult stands facing the child, knees flexed and feet apart. He grasps the child's wrists and the child steps up onto the adult, one foot on each thigh. The child leans back, as does the adult. (Sherborne 1990)

Double roll
The adult and child lie on their stomachs facing each other, grasping one another's wrists, and roll together over the floor or on a mat.

In her Developmental Movement Programme, Sherborne was concerned with developing several skills which are important to enable 'productive' conversational interchange. In 'with' relationships the adult encourages the child to become confident and as far as possible take an active, initiating and responsible role. The adult has to be aware of the need to play a responding role contingent upon the interests and desires of the child. He is encouraged to expand the movement initiations of the child, rather than to direct or control the child. In "against" relationships, attention, concentration and the ability to keep to the same movement are developed. Through movement the adult and child become involved in shared attention, which is identified as the basis for the development of shared meanings of words or symbols. (Wood et al 1987).

Participation in conversation demands knowledge of interpersonal and social skills. A partner cannot be too 'egocentric', he must be able to experience the situation from his listener's perspective (Wood et al 1987). Testing each other's strength in "against" relationships stimulates both partners to gain this sensitivity. In "shared" relationships the adult and child learn to cooperate as equal partners. This aspect is mentioned by many authors as a basic feature in the turn-taking process of "productive" conversation (Cazden, 1977, Lyon 1985, Wells 1984 and Wood et al 1987).

Conclusion

I started this presentation with Bronfenbrenner's statement that the most effective strategies of early intervention are those focusing attention on parent-child interaction around a common activity. Early parent-child interaction is recognised as one of the most powerful and favourable conditions for the child's development, due to intuitive parenting. The adult acts as a sensitive responder, adapting to the child's rhythm, signals and needs, feeding back experiences, interweaving and expanding them with their own responses.

The interaction context of disabled infants seems to be impaired by differences on the mother's part and the child's part. In the case of hearing impairment a typical interactional context is at risk and may impede the development of early conversational interchange, which is a basic component of language learning. SDM can be a joyful way for families with a young hearing-impaired child to experience and acquire communications skills. These skills are very important in the development of early conversational interchange and the natural communication rule comes into force if these are inhibited: "when communication breaks down, the powerful takes control" (Brinisch 1980).

References

Altshuler, K Z (1974) The social and psychological development of the deaf child: Problems, their treatment and prevention Am. Ann. Deaf.

Becwith, L (1977) Relationships between infants' vocalisations and their mothers' behaviours Merrill-Palmer Q.

Bonvillian, J D, Raeburn, V P, Horan, E A (1979) Talking to children: the effects of rate, intonation and length on children's sentence imitations J Child Lang.

Bowlby, J A (1989) A secure base. Clinical applications of attachment theory London: Tavistock/Routledge

Brinisch, P M (1980) "Childhood Deafness and Maternal Control" in Journal of Communication Disorders Vol 13, 1 pp.75-81

Bronfenbrenner, U (1974) "Is early intervention effective?" in Teachers College Record No: 76 pp279-303

Cazden, C B (1977) "Concentrated versus contrived encounters: suggestions for language assessment in early childhood education" in A Davies (Ed) Language and Learning in Early Childhood London: Social Science Research Council

Chadderton, J H, Tucker, I G and Hostler, M (1985) "The Responsiveness of Mothers of Young Hearing-Impaired Children to the Child's Communicative Initiations" in Journal of British Association Teachers of the Deaf Vol 9. 2.

Cheskin, A (1981) "The verbal environment provided by hearing mothers for their young deaf children" in Journal of Communication disorders 14 pp.485-496

Cheskin, A (1982) "The Use of Language by Hearing Mothers of Deaf Children in Journal of Communication disorders 15, pp.145-153

Collis, G M and Schaffer, H R (1975) "Synchronisation of visual attention in mother-child pairs" in Journal of Child Psychology and Psychiatry 16, pp315-320

Conti-Ramsden, G and Friel-Patti, S (1984) "Mother-child Dialogues: A Comparison of Normal and Language Impaired Children" in Journal of Communication Disorders

Conti-Ramsden, G and Friel-Patti, S (1986) "Mother-child dialogues: considerations of cognitive complexity for young language learning children" in British Journal of Disordered Communication 21, pp.245-255

Cross, T G (1977) Mothers' speech adjustments: the contribution of selected children: Language Input and Acquisition Cambridge University Press

Cross, T G (1978a) "Mothers' speech and its association with rate of language acquisition in young children" in _The development of Communication_ London

Cross, T G (1978b) _Mother-child interaction in the Study of Language development_ Doctoral dissertation, University of Melbourne

Cross, T G, Nienhuys, T G and Morris, J E (1980) _Maternal speech styles to deaf and hearing children_ Aust. T Deaf

Cunningham, C E, Reuler, E, Blackwell, J and Deck, J (1981) _Behavioural and Linguistic Developments in the Interaction of Normal and Retarded Children with their Mothers. Child Development_

Davis, H, Stroud, A and Green, L (1988) "The maternal language environment of children with language delay" in _British Journal of Disorders of Communication_ 23 pp.253-266

De Paulo, Bella, M and Bonvillian, J D (1978) "The Effect on Language Development of the Special Characteristics of Speech Addressed to Children" in _Journal of Psycholinguistic Research_

Drach, K U (1969) _The language of the parent: a pilot study. Working paper 14._ Language and Behaviour Research Laboratory, University of California, Berkeley

Ellis, R and Well, G (1980) _Enabling factors in adult-child language discourse_ First Language

Evans, A D (1975) _Experiential deprivation: Unresolved factor in impoverished socialisation of deaf school children in residence_ Amer. Ann. Deaf

Furrow, D, Nelsons, K and Benedict, H (1979) "Mothers' speech to children and syntactic development: some simple relationships" in _J Child. Lang_

Gardner, H (1989) "An investigation of maternal interaction with phonologically disordered children as compared to two groups of normally developing children" in _British Journal of Disorders of Communication_ 24 pp.41-59

Garnica, O K (1977) "Some Prosodic and Paralinguisitc Features of Speech to Young Children" in C E Snow and C A Ferguson (Eds) _Talking to children: Language Input and Acquisition_ Cambridge: Cambridge University Press

Goss, R N (1970) _Language used by mothers of deaf children and mothers of hearing children_ ADD

Goss, R N (1972) _Language used by mothers of deaf children and mothers of hearing children_ ASHA

Greenstein, J M, Greenstein, B B McConville, K and Stellini, L _Mother-Infant Communication and Language Acquisition in Deaf Infants_ Jackson Heights, NY: Lexington School for the Deaf

Gregory, S (1976) _Deaf children and their families_ Hearing

Hughes, M E (1983) "Verbal Interaction Between Mothers and their Young Hearing-Impaired Children in _Journal of British Association of Teachers of the Deaf_ Vol 7, 1 pp.18-22

Holzman, M (1974) <u>The verbal environment provided by mothers for their very young children</u> Merrily Palmer Quart

Kaye, H (1977) "Infant sucking behaviour and its modification" in L P Lipsitt and C C Spiker (Eds) <u>Advances in child development and behaviour</u> Vol 3. pp.2-52 London: Academic Press

Kaye, K (1977) "Toward the origin of dialogue" in H R Schaffer (Ed) <u>Studies in Mother-Infant Interaction</u> New York: Academic Press

Kogan, K L, Wimberger, H C and Bobbitt, R A (1969) <u>Analysis of mother-child interaction in young mental retardates</u> Child Development

Kretschmer, R R and Kretschmer, L W (1979) "The acquisition of linguistic and communicative competence: parent-child interactions" in <u>The Families of Deaf Children</u> Chapter 6 Volt. Rev.

Ling, D and Ling A H (1978) <u>Aural Habilitation: The Foundation of Verbal Learning in Hearing-Impaired Children</u> Washington: Alexander Graham Bell Association for the Deaf

Lyon, M (1985) "The Verbal Interaction of Mothers and their Pre-school Hearing-impaired Children: A Preliminary Investigation" in <u>Journal of British Association of Teachers of the Deaf</u> Vol 9. 5

Marshall, N, Hegrenes, J and Goldstein, S (1973) "Verbal Interactions: Mothers and their Retarded Children versus Mothers and their Non-retarded Children" in <u>American Journal of Mental Deficiency</u>

Meadow, K, Greenberg, M, Erting, C and Carmichael, M (1981) "Interactions of Deaf Mothers and Deaf Pre-school Children: Comparisons with Three Other Groups of Deaf and Hearing Children" in <u>American Annals of the Deaf</u>

Moerk, E L (1976) <u>Progress of Language teaching and training in the interactions of mother-child dyads</u> Child Development

Myklebust, H R (1964) <u>The Psychology of Deafness</u> 2nd Edition New York: Grune and Stratton

Newport, E L (1977) "Motherese: the speech of mothers to young children" in N Castellon, D Pisoni and G Potts (Eds) <u>Cognitive Theory Vol. 2</u> Hillsdale NJ: Lawrence Erlbaum Associates Press

Newport, E L, Gleitman, L and Gleitman, H (1975) "A Study of mothers' speech and child language acquisition" <u>Papers and Reports on Child Language Development</u> No.10 Stansford, Stansford University Press

Nienhuys, T G, Cross, T G and Horsborough, V M (1984) "Child Variables influencing maternal speech style Deaf and Hearing Children" in <u>Journal of Communicative Disorders</u> 17 pp.189-207

Philips, J (1973) <u>Syntax and Vocabulary of mothers' speech to young children: age and sex comparisons</u> Child Development

Papousek, H and Papousek, M (1983) "Biological basis of social interactions, implications of research for an understanding of behavioural deviance" in Journal of Child Psychology and Psychiatry 24, pp.117-129

Remick, H (1976) "Maternal speech to children during language acquisition" in W von Raffler-Engel, and Y Lebrun (Eds) Baby Talk and Infants' Speech Lisse, Netherlands, Swets and Zeitlinger

Rogers, S (1988) "Characteristics of social interactions between mothers and their disabled infants: a review" in Child. Care. Health and Development 14, pp.301-317

Sachs, J and Johnson, M L (1972) Language development in a hearing child of deaf parents Unpublished paper presented at the International Symposium on First Language Acquisition, Florence, Italy

Sachs, J (1977) The adaptive significance of linguistic input to prelinguistic infants Cambridge Mass. Cambridge University Press

Schaffer, H R, Collis, G M and Parsons, G (1977) "Vocal interchange and visual regard in verbal and pre-verbal children" in H R Schaffer (Ed) Studies in Mother-Infant Interaction New York: Academic Press

Schlesinger, H and Meadow, K (1972) Sound and Sign Berkeley, California: University of California Press

Schodorf, J K and Edwards, H T (1983) "Comparative analysis of parent-child interactions with language-disordered and linguistically normal children" in Journal of Communication Disorders 16, pp.71-83

Sherborne, V (1979a) "The significance of movement experiences in the development of mentally handicapped children" in G Upton (Ed) Physical and creative activities for the mentally handicapped Cambridge: Cambridge University Press

Sherborne, V (1979b) "Content of a development movement programme" in G Upton (Ed) Physical and creative activities for the mentally handicapped Cambridge: Cambridge University Press

Sherborne, V (1979c) "Movement for developmentally retarded children" in L Groves (Ed) Physical Education for special needs Cambridge: Cambridge University Press

Sherborne, V (1987) "Movement observation and practice, International perspectives in adapted physical activity" in Proceedings of the fifth International Symposium on Adapted Physical Activities Toronto, October 1-4, Champaign, Illinois, Human Kinetics Publishers Inc

Sherborne, V (1989) "Movement and the integration of exceptional children" in The Educational Forum Vol 54, 1

Sherborne, V (1990) Developmental Movement for Children Cambridge: Cambridge university Press

Simmons-Martin, A (1978) Verbal Learning Paper presented to Micha Society for Deaf Children, Tel Aviv, Israel

Snow, C E (1972) Mothers' speech to children learning language Child Development

Snow, C E, Arlman-Rupp, A, Hassing, Y, Jobse, J, Joosten, J, and Vorster, J (1976) Mothers' speech in three social classes J Psycholing

Snow, C E (1977) "The development of conversation between mothers and babies" in J Child Lang

Snow, C E and Ferguson, C A (Eds) (1977) Talking to children: Language Input and Acquisition Cambridge Mass.: Cambridge University Press

Snow, C E (1979) "Conversations with children" in P Fletcher and M Garman (Eds) Language Acquisition Cambridge: Cambridge University Press

Stern, B N (1974) "The mother and infant at play: the dyadic interaction involving facial, vocal and gaze behaviour" in M Lewis and L A Rosenblum (Eds) The effects of the Infant on his Care giver New York: Wiley

Trevarthen, C (1979) "Communication and co-operation in early infancy" in M Bullowa (Ed) Before Speech: The Beginning of Interpersonal Communication Cambridge: Cambridge University Press

Tucker, I G (1983) "The visual regard for mother of a group of hearing-impaired children reared using the auditory oral approach compared with a group of normally hearing children" in Journal of British Association for Teachers of the Deaf Vol 7. 1 pp.8-12

Vernon, M (1972) Psychodynamics surrounding the diagnosis of a child's deafness, Rehabilitation Psychology

Wells, G (1981) Learning Through Interaction: The study of Language Development Cambridge: Cambridge University Press

Wells, G (1984) Language Development in the Pre-school Years Cambridge: Cambridge University Press

Whitehurst, G J, Novak, G, and Zorn, G A (1972) Delayed Speech studied in the home, Developmental Psychology

Winicott, D W (1957) "Primary maternal preoccupation" in Collected papers: through paediatrics to psychoanalyses pp.300-5 London: Tavistock

Wood, D J (1980) "Teaching the young child: some relationships between social interaction, language and thought" in D Olson (Ed) Essays in Honor of J S Bruner New York: Norton

Wood, D, Wood, H, Griffiths, A, and Howarth, I (1987) Teaching and Talking with Deaf Children University of Nottingham

Chapter 7

Interaction processes in movement oriented intervention: A comparative study between developmentally delayed and normal children.

Cristian Dirjack

(Thesis submitted for the European Masters Degree in Adapted Physical Activity, Faculty of Human Movement, Technical University, Lisbon 1993)

Proceeding from a developmental psychopathological approach this investigation studied interaction processes of developmentally delayed children (ADD/H, attending a regular school) in three phase specific Relationship Situations (Relationship Play; Sherborne 1990) during their special physical education lessons. It followed three purposes;

a) the outline of a developmental and communicative model with respect to movement oriented intervention programmes;

b) the development of a reliable and valid observation instrument to assess communicative behaviour of children with ADD/H; and

c) the microanalysis of communicative behavioural modes of children with ADD/H vs. Non-ADD/H children (both ages 5 - 10) In three characteristically different movement relationship situations; (low-structured observation situations: 'cared', against, shared), in respectively a child-child dyad and a child-therapist dyad.

Hypothesis

The following hypothesis are better understood as 'working' hypotheses.

I.   Findings from the study of Wilcox, Kouri and Caswell (1990) lead to the assumption that the communicative and emotional behaviour of the child seems to be partner specific.

H0: The child's communicative behaviour in the low structured observation situation does not differ between a child-child dyad and a child-therapist   dyad.

H1: The child's communicative behaviour in the low structured observation situation differs between a child-child dyad and a child-therapist dyad.

II. The 3 different characteristic relationship situations; 'cared', 'against', 'shared' (CAS) reflect phase specific Relationship Situations in the course of a child's psychological development. Starting from the 'cared' relationship and swinging between the 'against' relationship characteristics and an increasing amount of the 'shared' relationship quality, the actual observed communicative behaviour points to the present stage of the development (Fig. 1).

H0: The Relationship Situations CAS do not differ significantly from each other.

H1: The Relationship Situations CAS differ significantly from each other.

III. Related characteristics of children with ADD/H promote retardations in several developmental areas such as cognitive (Safer & Allen 1976; Tarver-Behring, Barkley & Karlson,1985; Cantwell & Satterfield 1978), movement (Denclay & Rudel 1978), emotional (Weiss, Hechtman & Perlman 1978) and social ones (Johnston, Pelham & Murphy 1985; Pelham & Bender 1982; Milich & Landau 1982).

Poor peer acceptance and low capacity in creating and remaining in relationships are very common occurrences in children with ADD/H (Hubbard & Newcomb 1991; Clark, Cheyne, Cunningham & Siegel 1988; Landau & Milich 1988; Cunningham & Siegel 1987; Grenell & Glass 1987; Johnston, Pelham & Murphy 1985; Milich & Landau 1982: Pelham & Bender 1982). Different explanations were given by these authors. Examining patterns and the frequency of communicative behaviour and emotional expressions in the three characteristically different relationship situations will not only support the findings of previous studies (that of developmental relationships: in emotional and social skills in comparison to the control group) but further on provides important hints towards the implementations of early intervention programmes for those children: ·

a) in showing what current (developmental) level of relationship a rich child is able to perform;

b) by which preferred modes of communication; and

c) by uncovering latent capacities of the child's growth and change, valuable prognosis for treatment tenets could be established.

H0: Communicative Qualities and Communicative Modalities will not differ in the three relationship situations between children with ADD/H and Non-ADD/H children.

H1: Communicative Qualities and Communicative Modalities will differ in the three relationship situations between children with ADD/H and Non-ADD/H children.

oOo

a) In reference to the developmental psychological model from Kegan (1982) and the recent ideas from the multi perspective clinical development theory (Petzold 1992, 1993) a framework of the evolving self has been worked out that points out phase specific relationship characteristics which the child experiences in the continuity of his development. Concerning the communicative model, I refer to Zigmond 1987).

The Integrative Framework of the Evolving Self

It was mentioned in the introduction that this study pursues developmental psychopathological principles (including developmental variables in the research design). This approach requires a framework to which the results can be related. The framework presented here is called integrative because it represents the synopsis of psychopathogenetic as well as salutogenetic aspects in the continuity of the evolving self (Fig. 1).

48

Figure 1 shows the integrative framework of the evolving self

THE HELIX - this is figure 1

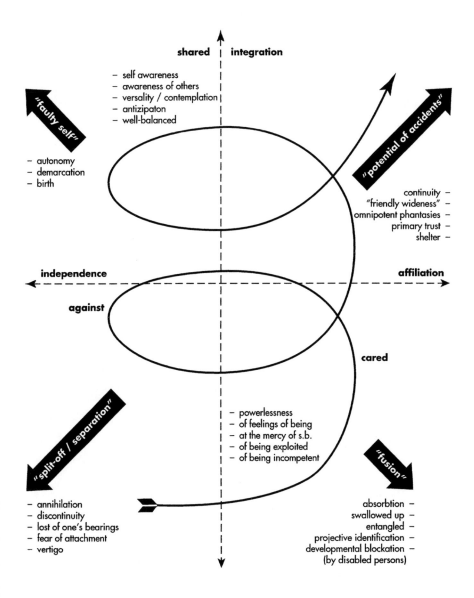

The idea of the helix here is derived from Kegan (1982 p.109 the `helix of evolutionary truces'). Kegan chose the symbol of the helix because it effectively illustrates the `balancing act' in which the evolving self has to encounter baffling psychological aspects that 'favours inclusion' (right side) and aspects of 'independence' (left side). Kegan describes 5 levels for the evolving self; 1. impulsive; 2. imperial; 3. interpersonal; 4. institutional; and 5. inter individual, and they are arranged on the 4 slopes (the outer points) of the helix, with the fifth level at its upper open end.

Three phase specific Relationship Situations (Sherborne 1990) fit into Kegan's helix (1982 : page 109) so far, a 'cared' and 'against' mark on the right and left sides of the illustration (the psychological aspects that he called `inclusion' and `independence'). The third Relationship Situation, 'shared', is supplemented here as an aiming integration of 'cared' and 'against' aspects into a well- balanced state. The tapering ascent of the helix signifies too this 'integrative' aspect. A supplement of Kegan's two dimensions, `inclusion' and `independence' (here represented by the horizontal line) is presented by the vertical line which adds a third dimension to Fig. 1. It integrates salutogenetic aspects of the evolving self by its 'shared'/integrative characteristics (upper attributions of the vertical line). At the base pathogenetic aspects are illustrated. In the corners of Fig. 1 four pathogenetic tendencies are represented; fusion, split-off/separation, faulty self[1], potential of accidents. Their attributions mark the line of demarcation (borderline) on the continuum between pathology and sanity.

b) The methodological part describes the research design and defines the observation instrument. The low structured observation situations (representing phase specific Relationship characteristics CAS) have been adopted from Sherborne's (1990) approach, "Developmental Movement for Children". Observation categories and determinants for the assessment of communication processes derived from Sarimsky (1986), Schlack (1989) and Wilcox et.al. (1990). Observed parameters in this study have been the Communicative Quality: interaction initiative, responsivity, pleasure and unpleasure; and the Communicative Modality: eye, body and verbal contact.

Figure 2 gives a graphical overview of the research design.

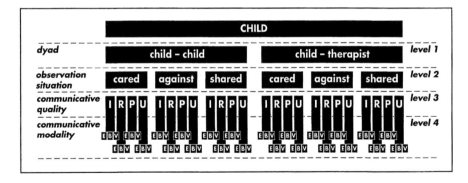

Figure 2: Schema of the data collection for a complete time sample for one child
(Respectively two minutes for any of the 6 observation situations of level 2)

---

[1] The four pathogenetic tendencies, I owe to a conversation with Hans von Luepke. The term 'faulty self' derived from Winnicott 1965.

Communicative Quality Level 3		Communicative Modality Level 4	
I	Interaction initiative	E	eye
R	Responsivity	B	body
P	Pleasure	V	verbal
U	Unpleasure		

Table O: Observed parameters and their items

The observation instrument showed inter reliability (r = .88). ANOVA of the 5 levels of the research design (O = group, 1 = dyad, 2 = low structured observation situation, 3 = communicative quality, 4 = communicative modality) yielded significance for level 2 = .0002; level 3 =.0001; level 4 = .0001. A supplementary factor analysis opened two factors for level 3 (separative and integrative), 2 factors for level 4 (cognitive and emotional) and one factor for level 5.

Discussion

Validity: The validity check, done by ANOVA and factor analysis permits statements about the construct validity of the research design. Interesting questions about the research design arose about the two dyad GROUPS; the child-child and child-therapist which led to my first hypothesis (H_1.) and the supposition of the three developmentally different relationship situations of CAS,which formed the basis of the low structured observation situations becoming my second hypothesis (H_2).

The two dyad groups did not show significantly different results for both groups, n = 13, as well as for respectively each group, the children with ADD/H and the Non ADD/H children. H_1 has to be refused. This finding is surprising as it does not confirm assumptions from Wilcox (1990) that:

> some children may be exposed to interactions in which their primary interactive partners are highly discrepant in their identification of and responses to the children's communicative behaviour (Wilcox et al 1990 p.691).

However, this statement could not be directly compared with the present investigation as Wilcox's primary purpose was the examination of partner-sensitivity of the communicative behaviour of young children (16 - 35 months). But the used items, EBV (eye, body, verbal contact) and their operationalisations have been the same and that is why, I argue, the supposition that the communicative behaviour of developmentally delayed children differ between interactions with a peer and a therapist. The present finding leads to the assumption that the 'general' communicative behaviour itself in on-task situations seems to be stable in regard to changing interaction partners as they were examined in this study. A look at the micro level of communicative behaviour however shows that differences of communicative qualities and communicative modalities occur within different dyads.

Table 1 Main effects of the four levels of the research design

level		F-value	F/M	p<
0	GROUP	0.17	0.72	n.s.
1	DYAD	0.40	1.12	n.s.
2	CAS	14.59	1.42	.0002
3	IRPU	45.99	1.29	.0001
4	EBV	116.90	2.69	.0001

n.s. = not significant   n = 13

Results of level 2, the relationship situation cared, against, shared, (C,A,S) showed a main effect (C-S p> .05, A-S p< .005, C-A p< .005). The ANOVA explain further which of the 3 variables C, A, S, were decisive for significant mean differences. H_0 of hypothesis II has to be refused.

Chart 1: Mean differences of level 2, the Relationship Situation

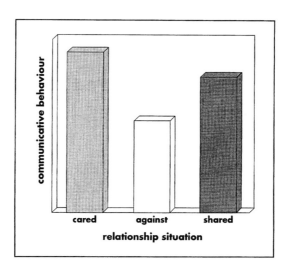

The relationship situation of 'cared' and 'shared' showed no significant mean differences. But the 'against' relationship situation shows significant mean differences (p< .005) in relation to 'cared' as well as to 'shared' (see chart 1 and table 2).

This result is quite interesting in regard to recent assumptions about the young child as an active and competent communication partner (Dorners 1993). In several observation studies from baby watchers (Petzold 1992 & 1993) it was seen that even the foetus already has at its disposal sharing qualities represented by skills for early communicative interactions with its environment (i.e. cue recognition, responsive as well initiating behaviour). The idea of the 'passive' young born with total dependence from his care givers and without any significant interaction skills fades more and more away. Chart 1 shows that the communicative behaviour, as it was assessed in this study, was high in 'cared' and 'shared' relationship situations and low in 'against' relationship situations. Within the context of the research design I have two comments to make: i) that the 'against' relationship situations did not primarily promote eye contact; but ii) eye contact is the most frequent communicative modality (See Chart 3). This means that the chance to show communicative behaviour in 'against' relationship situations was limited for the children in this investigation.

The results of the additional applied factor analysis support the recent understanding of young children's 'sharing' competency. Level 2, the relationship situations, opened two factors. The plot of factor pattern showed that the variables 'cared' and 'shared' lie on the same factor but on opposite sides, where as 'against' lies on a second factor. This suggests that the variables 'cared' and 'shared' tend to share some qualitative relationship characteristics, that I call here affiliation ("verschmelzen") whereas the variable 'against' represents a proper relationship characteristic. The helix Fig. 1 shows the three relationship characteristics. Affiliation on the right side represents the 'cared' relationship characteristic, independence on the left side the 'against' and integration in the upward tending direction the 'shared' one. The tapering ascent of the helix signifies the increasing integration of 'cared' and 'shared' characteristics. From its basic conditions are the 'cared' and the 'shared' relationship characteristic similar? Metaphorically expressed is the 'propogenetic competence' (Milani Comparetti/ Roser 1982, page 80) based in the 'seed' of the 'cared' property? This seed ripens in the course of a healthy and favourable development and develops the 'shared' quality of relationship characteristics by an integration of the originally 'cared' and 'against' relationship characteristics. Surely the active moments of the interaction of the baby are not yet conscious but 'mnemonic' (Petzold 1992, 1993). However, they have already at its disposal triggering and manipulating properties in regard to their environment (animate and inanimate). The assumption of the proper 'cared' relationship characteristic as the first quality of relationship in the development of the child, with an ongoing separation process by 'against' relationship situations, to later 'shared' ones needs a more differentiated consideration.

The 'cared' relationship characteristic is at the beginning characterised by an affiliation. In the on-going development, the 'cared' relationship characteristic will differentiate itself by experiences of 'against' relationship characteristics (i.e. of a higher level) in a way, that the 'cared' relationship characteristic now, will be set in relation to 'against' relationship characteristics and therefore becomes more conscious (reflexive); it becomes an integration. The child works out experiences of affiliation and independence in the course of its evolving self. At the beginning of the constitution of the identity they will get dynamically meaning attribution, which will, in the following developmental level, experience a respectively higher grade of consciousness (reflection) and therefore a higher grade of integration.

These experiences of affiliation and independence were described by Kegan (1982, 1991). A recent contribution from Petzold (1992, 1993) gives an overview of the field studies of the baby watchers and works out an integrated model of an early personal development under the new paradigm 'multi perspective clinical developmental theory' (in preference to the term 'developmental psycho pathology') because it represents better the synopsis of salutogenesis and pathogenesis (Petzold 1992, p.183/184)

The outcome of the ANOVA, as well as those from the factor analysis relativities and the sound assumptions from the psychoanalytical developmental theories that the child experiences different relationship situations in a linear developmental course of the evolving self, from 'cared' over 'against' to 'shared' relationship characteristics (as they have been simply called here). The findings of this investigation seem to support results from recent research that plead for sharing competencies for (even) the unborn and later baby, with the notion that these experiences get different meaning attribution along the continuity of the development.

Table 2:

ANOVA of the 4 levels of the research design

Variable	M		t(13)
6-5	0.18	1.86	.0879
AS	-0.41	-4.43	.0018
6-A	0.57	-5.72 (t(1 0))	.0003
1-R	0.36	1.10	.0737
1-P	0.18	1.14	.2808
1-0	1.30	10.26	.0001
R-P	-0.18	-1.18	.2658
R-U	0.94	13.11	.0001
P-U	1.12	8.48	.0001
E-B	2.06	13.67	.0001
E-V	1.80	11.71	.0001
B-V	-0.26	-3.07	.0118

Table 3: Factor analysis of variables of level 2, 3 and 4 of the research design

Variable	Factor 1	Factor 2	
cared	- 0.809	- 0.314	
against	- 0.001	0.945	level 2
shared	0.814	- 0.307	
	variance: 1.318	1.087	

Variable	Factor 1	Factor 2	
interaction			
initiative	- 0.856	- 0.266	
responsivity	0.961	0.029	level 3
pleasure	0.024	0.972	
unpleasure	0.819	- 0.157	
	variance: 2.330	1.055	

Variable	Factor 1		
eye	- 0.835		
body	0.736		level 4
verbal	0.678		

variance: 1.701

rotation method: varimax   n = 13

Level 3, the communicative quality interaction initiative, responsivity, pleasure and unpleasure (IRPU) showed significant mean differences. They were found for I (interaction initiative) versus U (unpleasure) p < .001, R (responsivity) versus U (unpleasure) p < .001 and P (pleasure) versus U (unpleasure) p < .001.

Chart 2: Mean differences of level 3, the Communicative Quality

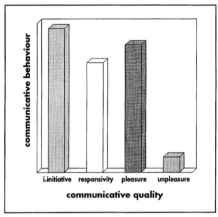

n = 13

The variable U is predominantly responsible for these mean differences. This result requires a careful interpretation. For the most part, the children did not show unpleasure behaviour. Therefore were the significant mean differences between I versus in U, R versus U and P versus U not so evident? A look on the group comparison (of level 3, the Communicative Quality elucidates why the variables I, R, and P did not yield significant mean differences for n=13.

The Communicative Quality of children with ADD/H seems not to be so differentiated as for Non ADD/H children. One could say that the depth (Greenspan 1984) of the Communicative Quality for children with ADD/H is not so marked as it is for their normal peers. Children with ADD/H did not bring into action their Communicative Quality in a such differentiated and intense way as the Non ADD/H children of this study. The Non ADD/H children on the other hand yielded significant mean differences of the Communicative Quality interaction initiative versus responsivity and responsivity versus pleasure. The results for the children with ADD/H neutralise the significant mean differences between interaction initiative, responsivity and pleasure for the Non ADD/H children so that for the total sample, n=1 3, no significant mean differences were obtained. An additional revelation gives the factor analysis of level 3, the Communicative Quality. The factor analysis opened 2 factors for the Communicative Quality (IRPU). On the plot of factor pattern lies I and R on one factor, but on opposite sides, where as P lies on a second factor. U lies somewhere near interaction initiative. The interpretation of this requires careful thought!

As mentioned before, the evidence of variable U is not so high. Therefore, the placement of variable U in the plot of factor pattern is somewhat accidental and could not be interpreted ingenious. (A similar outcome was seen in the factor analysis of level 2, the Relationship Situation). The variable interaction initiative and response seem to represent a similar communicative quality as where the variable pleasure clearly shows a different communicative quality. This leads to the assumption that the variables interaction initiative and responsivity can be understood as a more cognitive dimension of communicative quality, and the variables pleasure and unpleasure as a more emotional dimension. In the t-test calculations between the children with ADD/H and the Non-ADD/H children a combination of the variable I and R was applied to this cognitive dimension and a combination of P and U for this emotional dimension. Also the two dyad groups have been combined. Significant group differences were found for the interaction initiative - responsivity combination in an 'against' relationship situation t(12) = 3.148, p< .0104, herein the children with ADD/H showed the double of communicative behaviour than the Non-ADD/H children. For the variable combination P and U was found also significance in an 'against' relationship situation t(12) = - 3.039, p < .0125, but here it showed the Non-ADD/H children the double of the communicative behaviour of the children with ADD/H. An analysis of variance have not been applied to it. This short completion supports the assumption of the two dimensions of the communicative quality the cognitive and the emotional one.

Level 4, the Communicative Modality showed also a main effect. Each of the three modalities, eye (E), body (B) and verbal (V) differ significantly in their mean from each other. E versus B. p < .001, E versus V.p < .001 and B versus V p < .001.

Chart 3: Mean differences of level 4, the Communicative Modality

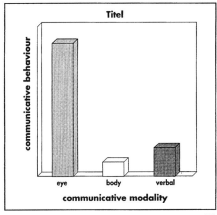

n = 13

It is clear to see, that eye contact was by far the most preferred Communicative Modality of the children in this investigation; that body contact gets the lowest rate of the three Communicative Modalities which lies in the observation situations itself. All observation situations included already initiated body contact which were not rated in the observations. Only the additional body contacts have been scored. Verbal contact or expressions have been rarely shown by the children.

Results of the application of the observation instrument of the study show differences in communicative behaviour in specific relationship situations between children with ADD/H and Non ADD/H children.

Chart 4: Significant group differences of communicative behaviour

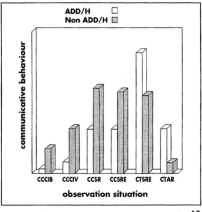

n = 13

Of importance were some significant results that were obviously influenced by the dyad. For level 3, the communicative quality, two significant group differences were found. Responsivity in a 'shared' relationship situation in a child - child dyad, p < .007, and responsivity in an 'against' relationship situation in a child -therapist dyad, p < .038. Chart 5 represents the results graphically. H_0 of hypothesis III has to be refused.

The different Dyads influenced the communicative behaviour of the children so that these findings do justify the design of the two dyad group, even though they did not yield significance in the ANOVA.

Chart 5: Significant group differences of level 3, the communicative quality.

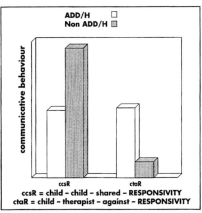

n = 13

The significant group differences represented in this chart cannot be interpreted in isolation. Important for the interpretation is that not only the relationship situation seems to play an important role for this outcome, but also level 2, the dyad. The 'shared' relationship situation was characterised by a simultaneous mutual dependence and mutual support. This characteristic requires an empathic quality towards the partner. Responsivity is one aspect of this empathic quality. The children with ADD/H in this study seemed to be overtaxed in handling issues of simultaneous mutual dependence with a peer. [However, in a child - therapist dyad of a 'shared' relationship situation they could show far more responsivity than the Non ADD/H children. That seems to be inconsistent! However, this comparison has to be seen in connection with the interaction initiative that the Non ADD/H children show in the same situation (child-therapist dyad) in relation to the children with ADD/H. Herein the Non ADD/H children show a high frequency of interaction initiative that correlates negatively with the responsive behaviour that yielded a low frequency under the same condition.]

Another effect is seen in the right hand of chart 5. This result may be influenced through level 2, the dyad. Herein the behaviour of the therapist in the 'against' relationship situation gains in importance. To get the children with ADD/H motivated in an 'against' relationship situation many interaction initiatives from the therapist were necessary. This illuminates the high frequency of responsive behaviour of the children with ADD/H for this observation situation.

Three other significant group differences were found for level 4, the Communicative Modality: i) Body contact, p < .005 and verbal contact, p < .003, as an interaction initiative in a 'cared' relationship situation of a child-child dyad (chart 6), and ii) eye contact, p < .05, as responsive behaviour in a 'shared' relationship situation of a child-child dyad and child-therapist dyad (chart 7). The first two results represent clearly the superiority in how the Non-ADD/H children make use of their range of Communicative Modalities in comparison to the children with ADD/H. They used far more body and verbal contact in this situation. The last two results have been influenced again by the dyad as the previous mentioned group differences of level 3, the Communicative Quality. Again, H0 of hypothesis III has to be refused.

Chart 6: Significant group differences of level 4, the Communicative Modality.

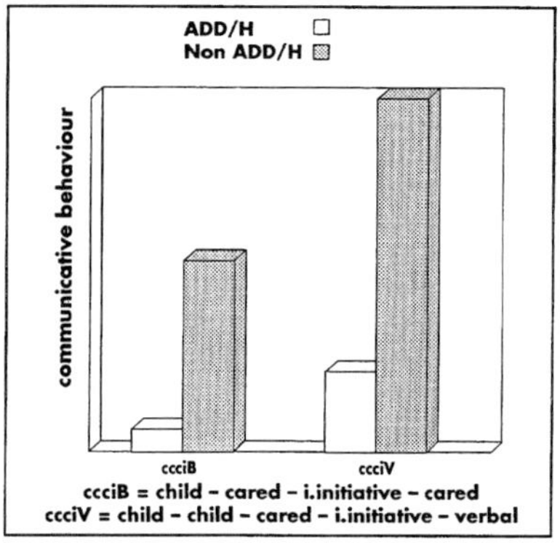

```
                    ADD/H      □
                    Non ADD/H  ▨

    communicative behaviour




              ccciB              ccciV
       ccciB = child - cared - i.initiative - cared
       ccciV = child - child - cared - i.initiative - verbal

                    n = 13
```

This chart represents clearly the superiority in how the Non ADD/H children make use of their range of Communicative Modalities in comparison to the children with ADD/H.

58

Chart 7 represents a similar effect as seen in Chart 6 for the right hand graph. Again, level 2, the dyad, influenced this result. The children with ADD/H show far less responsive behaviour through eye contact to their partners, as did the Non ADD/H children. The other way round is illustrated in the right hand graph, herein the children with ADD/H respond far more through eye contact to their partners (therapist), than did the Non ADD/H children. A similar explanation for this finding is described for chart 5.

Chart 7: Significant group differences of level 4, the Communicative Modality.

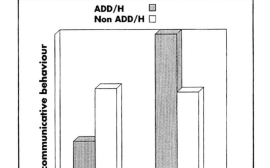

n = 13

Some potentially useful pedagogical and clinical recommendations can be selected from the present research. The complex research design in this study could be selected in isolated observation situations. The goal of the instrument lies in its further diagnostic oriented approach because the observation is done in movement oriented intervention usual relationship situations on a precise level of communicative behaviour (Communicative Quality, Communicative Modality). The observed communicative behaviour in each phase specific relationship situation gives not only information about the child's psychological development, but furthermore is the preferred Communicative Mode identified.

A second clinical recommendation lies in the application of this observation instrument for the evaluation of therapeutical aims. Therapeutical pre and post assessments can be helpful for evaluating the developmental progression. Another area that merits future investigative attention for Psychomotor Therapy (PMT) settings pertains to the relationship between the relationship situation 'cared', 'against', 'shared' and qualitative movement aspects. The KMP (Kestenberg Movement Profile, Kestenberg 1965, 1967, 1985; Lewis/Loman 1990) represents a sophisticated instrument in assessing developmental psychological stages in reflection of phase specific movement patterns.

Definition of Attention Deficit Disorder/Hyperactivity:

"ADD/H is a developmental disorder of attention span, impulsivity and/or over activity as well as rule-governed behaviour, in which these deficits are significantly inappropriate for the child's mental age; have an onset in early childhood; are significantly pervasive or cross-situational in nature; are generally chronic or persistent over time and are not the direct result of severe language delay, deafness, blindness, autism or childhood psychosis".

(Berkley R 1988; p.72: Attentional Deficit Disorder with Hyperactivity. In Mash, E J, and Terdal, C G (eds) Behavioural Assessment of Childhood Disorder 2nd Edition New York: Guildford Press)

References

Clark, M L, Cheyne J A, Cunningham, C E, Siegel, L S (1988) "Dyadic peer interaction and task orientation in attention deficit disordered children" in J. Abn. Child Psych 16:1 - 15.

Cantwell, D and Satterfield, H (1978) "The prevalence of academic underachievement of hyperactive children" in: J.o. Pediatr.. Psychology 3. p.168-71

Comparetti, M and Roser, L (1982) "Foerderung der Normaltaet und Gesundheit in der Rehabilitation" in M Wunder L Sierck Sie nennen a Fuersorge. Berlin.

Cunningham, C E and Siegel L. S.(1987) "Peer interactions of normal and attention deficit disordered boys during free play, cooperative task and simulated classroom situations" in: J. Abn. Child Psych. 15: p. 247 - 68.

Dorners, M (1993) Der kompetente Saeugling. Frankfurt. Fischer Taschenbuch.

Greenspan, S I and Porges, S W (1984) "Psychopathology in infancy and early childhood: clinical perspectives on the organisation of sensory and affective-thematic experience" in: Child Dev. 55. p. 49-70.

Grenell, M M and Glass, C R (1987) "Hyperactive children and peer interaction: Knowledge and performance of social skills" in: J. Abn. Child Psych. 15: p. 1 - 13.

Holtz, K L (1991) "Argumente fuer eine Ertwicklungstherapie" in: Psych. f.d. Praxis 5.

Johnston, C, Pelham, W E and Murphy, H (1985) "Peer relationships in ADD/H and normal children. A developmental analysis of peer and teacher ratings." in: J. of abnormal Child Psychology 71. p. 17-24.

Kegan, R (1982) The Evolving Self. Problem and Process In Human Development Cambridge: Harvard University Press

Kegan, R (1991) "Die Entwicklungsstufen des Selbst. Fortschritte und Krisen" im menschlichenLeben. Muenchen, Kindt Verlag.

Kestenberg, J (1966a) "The role of movement patterns in development: Rhythms of Movement" in: Psychoanalytic Quarterly 34a: pages 1-36.

Kestenberg, J (1965b) "The role of movement patterns in development: Flow of tension and effort" in Psychoanalytic Quarterly 34a: pages 617-83.

Kestenberg, J (1967) "The role of movement patterns in development: The control of shape" in: Psychoanalytic Quarterly 36: pages 366 - 499.

Kestenberg, J (1985) "The role of movement patterns in diagnosis and prevention" in D Shaskan and R William (Eds) Paul Schilder Mind Explorer pp.97 - 160. Human Science Press. New York.

Landau ,S and Milich, R (1985) "Social communication patterns of attention deficit disordered boys" in J. Abn. Child Psych. 16: pages 69 - 81.

Lewis, P and Lomans, S (1990) The Kestenberg Movement Profile. Its Past, Present Application and Future Directions. News Hampshire.

Pelham, W E and Bender, M E (1982) "Peer relationships in hyperactive children: Description and treatment" in: K Gadow & E Bialer (Eds) Advances in learning and behavioural disabilities. Vol.1, p. p. 366-436. Greenwich CT: JAI Press.

Petzold, H (1992a) Empirische Baby und Kleinkindforschung und der Paradigmenwechsel von psychoanalytischer Entwicklungspythologie und humanistischer psychologischer Unbekuemmertheit zu einer "mehrperspektivischen, klinischen Entwicklungspsychologie". Editorial; in: Integrative Therapie 18, 1: pages 1-11.

Petzold, H (1992b) Ein integratives Modell frueher Persoenlichkeittsevtwicklung als Beitrag " klinlscher Entwicklungspsychologie" zur Psychotherapie; in: Integrative Therapie 1: pages 66-96.

Petzold, H (1994) Psychotherapie und Babyforschung. Junfermann. Paderborn. In press.

Safer, R and Allen, D (1976) Hyperactive children. Baltimore Uni. Press.

Sarimsky, K (1986) Interaktion mit behinderten Kleinkindern. Muenchn. Reinhardt Verlag

Sarimsky, K (1991) Zur Beurteilung fruher kommunikativer Faehigkeiten entwicklungsverzoegerter Kinder; in: Fruehfoerderung interdiszipipinaer, 10, p. 151-59.

Schlack, H G (1987) "Die soziale Interaktion: Mittelpunkt therapeutischer Intervention zur Entwicklungsfoerderung behinderter Kinder" in O Speck , P Innerhofer and F Peterander [Hrsg.): Kindertherapie. Muenchen, Reinhard.

Tarver-Behring, S, Barkley, R. and Karlson, J (1985) "The mother-child interactions of hyperactive boys and their normal siblings" in: Amer. J. o. Orthopsychiatry, 55, p. 202-209.

Weiss, G, Hechtman, L, Perlman, T and Milroy, T (1985) "Psychiatric status of hyperactive adults: A controlled prospective 15 year follow-up of 63 hyperactive children" in J of Amer. Acad. Child Psychiatry 24: p. 211 20.

Wilcox, M J, Kouri, FA and Caswell, S (1990) "Partner sensitivity to communication behaviour of young children with developmental disabilities" in J. of Speech and Hearing Disabilities 66, p. 678-93.

Winnicott, D D (1965) "The maturational processes and the facilitating environment" New York. Dt.: Reifungsprozesse und foerdernde Umwelt. Muenchen 1974.

Zigmond, D (1987) "Three Types of Encounter in the Healing Arts: Dialogue, Didacticism and Dialectic" in Holistic Medicine 2 p. 69 - 81.

Part Two

Case Studies in

Sherborne Developmental Movement

Chapter 8

Eliciting Movement Patterns:
supporting perceptual motor abilities and general learning abilities; developing children as a whole.

Vesa Keskitalo

School Physical Education programmes must be developed

The starting point of my study was to look at Physical Education programmes in Finnish schools. I have been involved in Finnish School Physical Education as a teacher and a researcher for many years. As such I believe that a Finnish child does not receive a Physical Education programme that fully supports her development especially during the first two years of her life in school.

From my research I argue that during these first two years school Physical Education includes too many instances of inappropriate teaching and also too much emphasis on the more difficult skills and activities. The content and the difficulty level of the programme only meet the needs of the more able child and even then concentrates mainly on motor skill development. Further, the school Physical Education programme does not provide the appropriate level of physical and mental support that can be gained from the right kind of movement experience. Too many children learn at the very beginning to fear the failure that can come from learning skills that are too difficult. From this they also find their social position in the classroom hierarchy, the best, the average and those who are not so good. If they only learn to fail then they loose their self assurance before it has been developed through positive movement experience. Beyond this there is often no recognition for the potential to support the general learning ability of the child through an effective movement programme.

If we want a movement programme to support children's physical and mental development it must influence the right aspects of movement learning. Above all the level of difficulty level must match the ability of the child, for example, not too difficult to prevent effective movement. Thus we have the possibility of enabling the children to develop through a more holistic experience.

We try to improve both moving abilities and general learning abilities

We all know that perceptual-motor development plays an important role in cognitive functioning and developing the 'readiness skills'. As the child moves in her surroundings she perceives her environment and analyses her movements in relation to time, space, dynamics and relationships which, I argue, is the basis of all learning. Moving is essential when children build up physical perceptions of themselves, their understanding of the immediate environment and the world around them. During early school years movement still is one of the primary stimuli by which they grasp fundamental cognitive concepts of direction, space, time, peer relations and their self-image. These factors are necessary for all learning. In addition to this we must take into consideration that, at the age of 6-7 years, their basic ability to think at a sophisticated level is not fully developed which makes it difficult for them to learn through formal means of education. Perceptual motor abilities and general readiness for learning are still closely interrelated during the preschool and primary years. Thus, we have the potential to influence the general learning ability of the child, for example though movement observation, analysis, decision-making and moving again.

Although we know that in some cases lack of readiness skills is the result of inadequate maturation, more often lack of readiness skills is due to inadequate movement experiences and learning before school age. There can be at least some potential to try to improve these abilities if early opportunities for the children have been previously inhibited or retarded.

Easy basic movements: a way to perceptual motor development

I believe that to vary a single movement within a movement experience lesson makes that movement much more effective. For example, setting out obstacles over a running course at irregular intervals gives a variety of challenges to the child's perceptual motor function as she runs. If this movement experience is considered immediately after completion, through appropriate feedback, then the process of perception directs the effects to the basic elements of the perceptual motor functions.

In such situations the sensory stimulation functions of the child are under heavy loading and, provided there is no overloading, the benefits can be profound. The child evaluates the movement experiences internally, may talk about them and then moves in the way the situation and their thoughts determine. For the teacher, this makes demands on programme planning because, for example, overloading for the child can be caused by presenting movement tasks that are too difficult. When the move is familiar then every child <u>dares</u> to participate and can perform the task in her way. This process of match and differentiation is vital and, I argue, one that the traditional and inflexible Finnish teaching system does not facilitate.

Children are differently developed

Young children in the early years of their education have a wide range of motoric ability. Some children are not even near the maximal level of their movement potential because of their minimal movement experiences. Those whose movement experience is more extensive and versatile can move in quite sophisticated ways. When a young child is 'normally' developed and her movement experience is perfect then her basic movement experiences can be varied, for example, by asking:

* is the use of power appropriate for the movement (all parts of the body);
* can the dynamic quality be varied?
* do the parts of the movement join together fluently and is the timing accurate?
* does the whole body move in a natural rhythm that the movement demands?
* is direction of the movement (the spatial quality) appropriate (the body and its parts) and does it have variety within space?
* is the movement in balance?

This principle may well be applicable to all children. From my research, I argue that children often are lacking in their basic movement competence if we compare it with the ideal movement described above. All these qualifying attributes above describe the directions that I believe Physical Education programme planning should take.

Varying movement is important - a child can vary Movement Patterns

When the child is competent and confident with basic movement then they can be asked to introduce variety. As a teacher our responsibility is to give movement tasks that require the child to use her perceptual senses in an accurate and quick way. Though this puts the whole perceptual motor ability area under heavy loading I believe it is important for learning that the child is challenged. She can be asked to vary the speed, strength, rhythm, direction etc of her movement. However, this is not possible when we use movements which are new, which must be learned and which are too difficult. I am not saying that we must reject the teaching of new skills, I only stress the importance of using basic movement patterns in the Physical Education programme for first year pupils. Easy movements also provide the potential for every child to succeed and so we do not destroy their self assurance at the very beginning.

All children need training in Movement Patterns

The average early years child can walk, run, hop... and perform several other simple basic movements quite well. My research shows, however, that the interpretation of these movement patterns by the children is quite narrow. With only a little effort we can get all the children to move in a much more sophisticated way. The less able the children are then the greater the potential to improve their movement abilities - of course related to their skill level.

The quality of movement is extremely important

This has led me to the conclusion that these simple movement experiences must be emphasised in the Physical Education programme. This is vital if we want to influence the perceptual motor development of the children and to therefore teach in a more holistic way. Movement observation, by the teacher and by the child, should be a central part of the lesson and the learning experience. The observation skills of the child and the development of their perceptual motor ability should not be left to chance. However, it is important to remember that we cannot do all this with difficult and new movements. In this case all the learning energy concentrates on the new movement itself, and the child is not able to make the observations and improvements.

If movement experiences are presented to the child in an easy way, slowly, without changing rhythm or direction, etc., it is ineffective. We do not get the effects we want on the child's overall development, neither do we teach them either to move or to develop mentally. The quality of the first year Physical Education programme is extremely important for children's development. Poor quality teaching and learning can destroy the self assurance of the child.

I accept that we do not know the extent to which perceptual motor training supports other ability areas to promote, for example, specific readiness for schoolwork. However, I believe that the enhancement of body, spatial, directional and temporal awareness is a way of guiding a child towards improved movement control and efficiency in fundamental movement and is valuable in itself. If we want to achieve such learning results and more, like developing self assurance, we are obliged to use movement activities with which the children are familiar. Movement activities for living not for sports - although both can be catered for by the school.

To the final end

My sincere aim is to improve the school Physical Education programme. If I can find some connections that improve also the general learning experience for children in the Finnish School system I will be quite satisfied. The main idea is that the child is taught as a whole person. Sherborne Developmental Movement will be used to develop my ideas during the research experiment which starts in 1996.

References

Gallahue, D (1982) _Understanding motor development in children_ John Wily and Sons. New York

Godfrey, B and Kephart, N C (1969) _Movement Patterns and Motor Education_ Appleton-Century-Crofts: New York

Keskitalo, V (1994) _Uuteen yleisurheilun opetukseen. Spurtti_ 3/1994, 4-5

Sherborne, V (1990) _Developmental Movement for Children_ Cambridge University Press

Chapter 9

Enabling primary school teachers to teach through Sherborne work

Steve Mellor

As part of the Physical Education Research programme at the University of Plymouth I am currently involved in a project investigating the teaching of Physical Education by non-specialist Physical Education teachers in primary schools. The project examines the support currently available to these teachers and compares this to their perceived in-service support needs. The decision to initiate this research project developed from my teacher training days where, as a Physical Education student on a primary BEd programme, I experienced a curriculum leadership placement in a primary school. My brief was to develop my own curriculum leadership skills in Physical Education and to help implement a programme of activity in an aspect of the Physical Education National Curriculum which the school identified as requiring support. Further teaching experience, and day to day conversation with colleagues in schools have focussed my thoughts more precisely on the contentious issue of effective school and curriculum management in the current economic climate. This has directed me towards examining the support needs of colleagues in curriculum areas where they see themselves as 'non-specialists'.

I argue that the consensus view held by the teachers within my research community in primary schools shows a level of insecurity in teaching primary Physical Education. When engaging in debate about the nature and purpose of Physical Education many teachers state that it is only a physical activity. Consequently, teachers teach only the physical dimensions and often neglect a more holistic approach (Dibbo and Gerry 1995). However, other teachers demonstrated an awareness of the potential of the hidden curriculum but were generally unable to manage such learning as they were constrained by their dualistic perception of Physical Education. Hargreaves points out that the hidden curriculum is broadly the same for all pupils and affects them in the same way (1982, p.10). The hidden curriculum is taken to mean those things not necessarily intentionally taught, for example the aesthetic, personal, social and moral development which are culturally valued aspects of education, but are intrinsic to the Physical Education lesson.

The following story provides a practical illustration for the theoretical discussion:

A close friend began her teaching career last year and she admitted to me that she avoided physical activity if at all possible. Like many primary school teachers she found herself having to take Physical Education lessons twice a week in order to fulfil her contractual obligations. During her time as a student she had endured my debate about how important Physical Education is to the development of the whole child and has, she felt, gained a greater understanding of the nature of Physical Education .

During her last teaching practice she used Sherborne Developmental Movement (SDM) with her year one class having asked me to write lesson plans for her use. The teaching practice lessons went well and her confidence grew. Given a reception class in her first teaching post, she decided again to use SDM as the framework for her teaching of Physical Education in the first term. She found that this formed an excellent base both for her and her pupils as they built relationships and worked together in school.

We have since talked about her current work and the work of her colleagues, especially the issues raised by the work of her colleague in the parallel reception class. This teacher had adopted what she thought was the easy option and introduced apparatus work in term one with the following results;

1. The children now associate Physical Education with using apparatus and are disappointed when it was not used;

2. The teacher encountered organisational problems as the children found difficulty in working together;

3. Safety factors were raised as the children were unaware of their bodies and individual limitations;

4. Minimal engagement in physical activity occurred as they were unable to co operate effectively when organising the apparatus;

5. Instruction and language was used to maintain discipline rather than teach.

In contrast, my friend and colleague has expressed the enjoyment that she and the children have gained from her Physical Education lessons. SDM has given her the opportunity to work with the children in a safe environment and the development of positive relationships between herself and the children, and between the children themselves, has enabled her to concentrate her energies on working with the class rather than against them. When she introduced simple apparatus in the second term the childrens' knowledge of their own strengths and weaknesses was apparent. They exercised responsibility and would climb on the apparatus, however, if they felt this was too difficult for them they could manage the situation and return to a less difficult task. Language acted as a key to extend their movement education as they were able to experience concepts such as 'through', 'over', 'under', 'pushing' and 'pulling'. Their language evolved to naming body parts and describing the dynamics of movement eg; what , how, where and with whom. As their relationships developed so the children started to look after each other as they built trust. This is a key element in SDM as for example, one child takes their partner for a journey around the room by gently pushing them back to back.

Therefore, for these children, Physical Education had become a fun session in which they worked with others rather than against them. Their communication skills were enhanced as they expressed their feelings and experiences and they began to discover what their bodies could and could not do in a safe, yet demanding way. SDM set the scene and created a theme for the second two terms and was instrumental in establishing clear teaching structures which were transferable to other areas of the Physical Education curriculum.

Analysis

SDM is an approach to Physical Education which enhances an individuals awareness of their body. It also has the potential to develop self awareness and promote a positive body image, it can develop an awareness of others and build meaningful relationships (Sherborne 1990). Therefore I argue, SDM has tremendous potential for all children not just children in special education. Through a combination of factors it also has great potential for teachers by offering a clear framework from which they can work. Firstly, it enables teachers to change their perspectives of Physical Education is and should be; secondly, it enhances the confidence of the teacher to teach Physical Education; and thirdly it develops language skills and positive relationships which provide the teacher with control in a safe and caring environment, thus bringing more than just the physical dimension to the learning within the Physical Education lesson ie; the hidden curriculum.

70

The National Curriculum for Physical Education non-statutory guidelines outline some of the features which SDM hopes to promote. It states that:-

1.2   Physical education can also contribute to :
a   the development of problem solving skills;
b   the establishment of self-esteem through the development of physical confidence; and
c   the development of inter-personal skills.   (Section B1)

I argue that by employing SDM we do contribute to the areas identified by the National Curriculum for Physical Education and therefore, work towards developing the whole child. This method acknowledges the children and the impact of the delivery of the curriculum and the hidden curriculum all of which has a major influence on pupil attitudes to Physical Education (Fox 1989). In fact, pupil attitude to Physical Education is most influenced by the things that we can do something about ie; the way we teach and what we teach (Tinning 1987). Therefore by utilising SDM a more sensitive teaching of Physical education can be achieved.

> . . teaching better must include getting inside the hidden curriculum. The responsibility for the hidden agenda of our teaching must rest with us as teachers. We must attempt to understand what hidden messages are being conveyed in our Physical Education teaching. When we have this realisation we must challenge the taken-for-granted in such messages and actively try to change in ways that make our teaching more sensitive and less destructive (p.107).

Where the problem initially lies

Fox (1988) believes that people on leaving secondary school fall into 3 psychological categories with respect to physical activity;

1. the approachers -'Those who perceive some kind of reward in sport and/or exercise and who actively and independently seek out physical experiences'; (p.35)

2. the avoiders - 'Those who perceive sport and/or exercise as a potentially negative experience, and who are unlikely to be seriously involved again for the rest of their lives, without substantial persuasion'; and (p.35)

3. the neutrals - 'Those who have no strong feelings about sport and/or exercise, and whose activity patterns are probably more dependent on social and environmental circumstances than strong convictions' (p.35).

Physical Education in secondary education is taught by specialists, people who have chosen to teach Physical Education full-time (Templin 1988) and therefore, is almost certainly taught by those in the approachers category for, if they were not approachers then they would not have chosen to pursue study and work in that area (p 60-70). However, this same theory does not apply to primary education. Primary Physical Education may be taught by approachers, the avoiders, and the neutrals (Mellor 1994 M Phil thesis in progress). This leads me to suggest that there are at least three reasons why teaching Physical Education in primary schools should be approached from a quite different perspective than the way Physical Education is taught in secondary schools:

1. Teachers represent all three categories in primary education resulting in contrasting enthusiasms;
2. There is an obvious disparity between time spent in training primary school teachers to teach Physical Education and time spent in training secondary teachers to teach Physical Education; and

3. resources for Physical Education may not be a high priority in already overstretched primary school budgets.

I feel that SDM is accessible to primary teachers for several reasons; it does not require apparatus yet provides opportunities for activities such as rolling, falling, transferring weight, locomotion and partner work, allowing children to discover different things that their bodies can do; it enables children to have the opportunity to focus their strength by pushing or pulling their partner; and it enables children to have the opportunity to experience sensations such as flow, initiated by someone else for example, 'rocking' activities (Sherborne 1990). SDM clearly emphasises the cognitive as well as the physical dimensions through developing relationships, concept development, language development and communication skills. I feel that this offers a framework for primary teachers to help them feel comfortable and secure teaching in the Physical Education environment.

The effect of shifted emphasis

A predominant view of the teachers I interviewed in primary education suggests that sport and Physical Education are inextricably linked. The following example illustrates this perspective:

> We have a responsibility to encourage healthy attitudes towards physical activities - our main job is to make sports etc. fun - so that they're more likely to maintain interest in sports etc;, later in life (Mellor 1994 - extract from an interview with a primary school teacher).

However, I challenge this view and, as others (Williams 1989, Chappell 1988), see sport and Physical Education as separate entities, yet containing common physical ingredients which creates a link between them at the primary stage of schooling. Nelligan (1991) believes that Physical Education and sport are, and should remain, quite separate and distinctive areas within the school environment, a view supported by Wilcox (1980). He stresses that a separation of Physical Education and sport is the only solution to ensure maximum fulfilment for both parties. However, the dichotomy that he refers to does not exist in the reality of the lifeworld of primary school teachers, for example football and netball are still taught with adult rules in an alarming number of schools. Nevertheless, it can be argued that sport does contribute to Physical Education as in the case of swimming where 'many of the rules enable the average swimmer to perform their swimming strokes more proficiently' (HCC Swimming 1989 p.77) if the relationship between Physical Education and sport is managed effectively. For example, the Halliwick method (Stewart 1990 p.21-23) of swimming, encourages children to develop water confidence and the ability to swim through a discovery based learning approach. It fosters independence by relying on the natural buoyancy of the water and, although incorporating the prescribed strokes set down by the Sports National Governing Body the physical dimension is only one of the aspects of this teaching method.

Sport and Physical Education are multi-faceted and to use the terms interchangeably has inherent dangers. I make this strong claim because I believe that the media presents us with powerful images of aggression, self-interest and winning at all costs. This portrayal emphasises values which I feel should not become part of Physical Education's hidden agenda. Alternatively by creating Physical Education programmes which concentrate on developing the childrens' self-esteem, interpersonal skills and the teacher's awareness of the power of the hidden curriculum, these negative values may be avoided. As such, by using SDM within programmes of work for primary Physical Education, the teacher can develop more than just a sport and physical skills based curriculum.

> The outward and visual signs must be attended by an inward and spiritual grace if Physical Education is to be considered as having taken place' (Morgan 1974 p.3).

So, if Physical Education and sport are separate entities (Nelligan 1991) which project diverse messages, a consideration of the meaning of Physical Education is required.

A theoretical framework

In attempting to analyse Physical Education in terms of its status and role within the educational process, Arnold (1979) uses a framework in which physical activity, or movement, is seen to have three dimensions of educational significance:

     (i)   education **IN** movement
     (ii)   education **THROUGH** movement
     (iii)   education **ABOUT** movement

Education IN movement recognises the belief that physical activities are in and of themselves worthwhile, something which can only be fully appreciated through participation. A child who is not adept in reading skills by the time she goes to secondary school may be disadvantaged for the rest of her life. In the same way a child who is not adept in physical skills by that age may also be disadvantaged for the rest of her life (Whitaker 1984 p.7).

This is the intrinsic dimension of Physical Education; the management and expertise of body movement and skills acquisition.

> ... by giving the child the experience of movement activities, we are introducing him/her to a 'physical' dimension which should be included in education for its intrinsic value and for the satisfaction which such movement experience can bring (Williams 1989 p.21).

Physical activities are not by their very nature educational but they do possess educational potential. Physical Education is not just a collection of physical activities, but rather a kind of education that is 'education through movement' or 'education through the physical' (Morgan 1974 p 3).

In education THROUGH movement Arnold recognises the value of Physical Education in achieving those educational objectives which are not an intrinsic part of physical activity. This is the hidden curriculum, with objectives such as aesthetic, personal, social and moral development which are culturally valued aspects of education.

Education ABOUT movement acknowledges the need to study concepts, rules and procedures and is thereby concerned with understanding and intelligent performance e.g. the benefits of exercise or teamwork. Both Health Related Fitness (HRF) and Teaching Games for Understanding (TGFU) are underpinned by beliefs in the importance of education about the physical. These two innovations, along with concepts such as Sport for All, Active Life Styles (ALS) and mixed sex grouping, constitute the 'new' Physical Education which '...challenges both content and pedagogy, claiming greater accessibility, equality and egalitarianism' (Thomas 1989 p.6). I agree with Williams (1989) when she states that;

> ...if Physical Education is to achieve its potential as an educational medium, the curriculum must be planned so that a range of objectives is included. It is not enough simply to expose children to various physical activities and hope that a whole host of outcomes will automatically ensue (p.24).

Physical Education consists of more than just sport or recreation. It is not just an 'opportunity to let off steam'. Through effective teaching which develops the skills of learning alongside the intended motor competencies and encourages self-evaluation, the teacher and learner will be involved in Physical Education in its fullest form (Connell 1989 p.118).

For many class teachers, the teaching of Physical Education is loaded with organisational hassles and, in the interests of making the job easier, maintaining control by means of controlling all the decisions seems well justified. Yet there is a paradox here. Maintaining control in this manner is an act requiring vigilance, and maintaining vigilance is a stressful activity (Tinning 1987 p.103).

I suggest that SDM allows children to be given more responsibility for their own learning which in fact reduces the stress experienced by teachers(1987). Tinning believes that if all decisions are made by the teacher the cumulative effect of this dependence on the teacher is that students will become unable to work independently of the teacher's organisation and direction. Kutnick (1988) shows that teachers in Physical Education lessons demonstrate an overwhelming concern for pupil behaviour. Instead of focusing on the physical and intellectual needs of the pupils they place themselves in a situation of control and management, not only of the actions of their pupils but also their interactions.

My research suggests that primary schools are places where, in Physical Education lessons, teachers maintain traditional use of didactic practices, much of the discourse is used to communicate classroom authority, most statements about learning and social activity are about control. Although there are many examples of group work there are few examples of genuine co-operation and pupils themselves do not strive for independence but refer to their teacher for decisions and support concerning simple and complex learning. Tinning (1987) argues that teachers have a role in promoting autonomy through Physical Education and to do so needs recognition of the overt and hidden curricula. They need to change their role from peer to partners to avoid hierarchical constraints on pupils and need to structure social experience to allow co-operative alternatives to be effective.

Before concluding I will leave the reader with a second practical illustration to reinforce some of the points I have raised in this discussion. This example is taken from my own work in schools:

I was asked by the teacher of year six children to take a lesson concentrating on bat and ball skills. The teacher warned me that the children were unable to cooperate and he told me that I should 'come down hard on them if they started to mess about'. I considered that instead of addressing the issue of relationships and cooperation the teacher had concentrated on the skills aspect of the curriculum rather than directing his attention towards the hidden curriculum. In reality he had made his job harder.

After working through some warm-up and stretching exercises with the children, I decided to introduce some SDM activities as a further warm-up and an introduction to the lesson. Sliding each other, prisons, blind walk and back to back, finally they were asked to remain sitting back to back resting against each other. I handed a ball to each pair and asked them to turn around, still sitting and with legs apart, feet touching their partners and to start rolling the ball to each other. Activities were then extended whereby they moved further apart and onto their feet, throwing the ball to each other at first then batting it with their hands and finally via targets on the floor. I finished the lesson with another SDM activity of sticking to the floor as I walked around seeing if I could lift parts of their body from the floor, after which they all stood up quietly and lined up to return to the classroom.

Conclusion

On explaining this lesson to a fellow Physical Education student while bouncing around ideas for this paper it was interesting to note his initial reaction: Was I advocating that something as important as SDM should merely be used as a warm-up and cool down activity in mainstream primary education? This is definitely not the case. The SDM in this lesson was used by me to bring the hidden curriculum to the fore. By utilising the cognitive, social and affective dimensions implicit within SDM I moved beyond the physical skills teaching which is explicit within most Physical Education lessons. I was able to create a framework to initiate a theme of partnerships and cooperation which continued throughout the whole lesson and not only whilst engaged in SDM activities. I therefore suggest that SDM is a tool which gives teachers in primary education a chance to re-evaluate what Physical Education can be and should be. It enables them to teach through the hidden curriculum as well as teaching 'in', 'through' and 'about' movement.

References

Arnold, P J (1979) Meaning in Movement, Sport and Physical Education London: Heineman

Chappell, R (1987) "School sport in Great Britain" in Bulletin of Physical Education Vol.23 No. 3 Winter

Chappell, R (1988) "Role of the Physical Education teacher - revisited" in Bulletin of Physical Education Vol 24 No. 3 Winter

Connell, R (1989) in A Williams (Ed) Issues in Physical Education for the primary years Lewes: The Falmer press

DES (1992) Physical Education in the National curriculum London: HMSO

Dibbo, J and Gerry, S (1995) "Physical Education: Meeting the Needs of the Whole Child" in The British Journal of Physical Education Spring 1995

Fox, A (1988) "The child's perspective in Physical Education" pts 1-6 in The British Journal of Physical Education Vol. 19 No. 1 - Vol. 20 No.1

Hargreaves, D (1982) The Challenge for the comprehensive School: Culture, Curriculum and Community London: Routledge and Kegan Paul

Hertfordshire County Council (1989) Swimming

Kutnick, P (1988) Relationships in the primary school classroom Paul Chapman Publishing Ltd, London

Mellor, S (1994) M Phil research project (still in progress)

Morgan, R E (1974) Concerns and values in Physical Education London: Bell and Sons Ltd

Nelligan, C (1991) "Physical education and sport: are they compatible?" in Bulletin of Physical Education Vol. 27 No. 2 Summer

Sherborne, V (1990) Developmental Movement for Children Cambridge: Cambridge University Press

Stewart, D (1990) The Right to Movement Basingstoke : The Falmer Press

Templin, T (1988) "Settling down: An examination of two Physical Education teachers" in J Evans (Ed) Teachers Teaching and Control in Physical Education Lewes: Falmer Press

Tinning, R (1987) Improving Teaching in Physical Education Deakin University, Sydney

Whitaker, K (1984) "Introduction & Primary school physical education : The way ahead" in M Mawer and M Sleap (Eds) Physical Education within Primary Education University of Hull, L&T Press Ltd

Wilcox, R (1980) "PE or Sport" in British Journal of Physical Education, 11 (6)

Williams, A (1989) Issues in Physical Education for the Primary Years Lewes: The Falmer Press

Chapter 10

Sherborne Developmental Movement
&
Gymnastics in the Primary School

Linda Mongey

Introduction

For my BEd thesis I decided to research into the significance of relationship play[1] in developing gymnastic skills. This project was greatly influenced by the innovative teaching ideas of Veronica Sherborne who strongly believed that children have two basic needs; i) they need to feel at home in their bodies; and ii) they need to be able to form safe and caring relationships with others. I wanted to investigate whether the fulfilment of these needs can be achieved through the relationship play activities developed by Sherborne. These activities are designed to encourage children to explore and discover movement through co-operation, enabling children to develop body knowledge, movement and relationship skills (Sherborne 1990, p.v).

I taught relationship play lessons at two local mainstream primary schools with two classes, each class having an average of thirty children aged between nine and eleven years old. The data I gathered focussed on how these learning experiences can provide a basis from which children can develop gymnastic skills and the factors which may influence this skill acquisition. My research has suggested that this was achieved in two distinct ways; i) through children using their bodies as apparatus; and ii) through children experiencing and performing gymnastic skills beyond their perceived abilities. It is the intention of this paper to discuss how these two factors play a significant role in developing the learning and performing of gymnastic skills.

Skill development through relationship play

To understand how relationship play can help to develop the learning and performing of gymnastic skills I will first consider the notion of 'skill'. According to Whiting this refers to;-

> Complex, intentional actions involving a whole chain of sensory, central and motor mechanisms which through the process of learning have come to be organised in such a way as to achieve predetermined objectives with maximum certainty (in Mace and Benn 1982, p.88).

Therefore, skill acquisition in gymnastics encompasses both perceptual and motor responses which are acquired through learning (Mace and Benn 1982, p.88). Such responses are integrated and organised into movement patterns to achieve a predetermined goal with precision, accuracy and quality. However, the term skill is often confused with the term ability and Sage clearly distinguishes between these two terms when he states;

> ...abilities serve as foundation stones for the development of skills which are specific responses for the accomplishment of a task (p.88/89).

---

[1] Relationship play uses three basis types of relationship, 'with', 'against' and 'shared'. These types are described by Gerrit Loots in Chapter 4 of this book.

In gymnastics a skill is learned through continuous repetition and practice and depends on the presence of underlying abilities (Sage in Mace and Benn 1982 p.89) such as flexibility, stability and co-ordination. Skill acquisition in gymnastics may therefore depend on whether children have experienced or developed the five movement abilities identified in the Physical Education National Curriculum; jumping, rolling, balancing, suspending one's weight (eg; hanging) and taking weight on hands (DES 1992, p.5). Development of ability in each of these movement areas can provide a sound basis from which children can develop gymnastic skills. However, learning these gymnastic skills may become secondary to other types of learning which take place such as decision making, spatial awareness and body awareness.

Relationship play and it's contribution to holistic development

Relationship play provides opportunities for children to explore their bodies, developing body awareness. Gallahue (1980) defines body awareness as the ability to differentiate between body parts, enabling the children to gain an understanding of the nature of the body (p.333). This awareness of the body develops in three areas:

1. Knowledge of the body parts;
2. Knowledge of what the body parts can do; and
3. Knowledge of how to make the body parts move.

Such awareness of the body Sherborne (1990) believes enables children to develop a sense of wholeness (p.4), an understanding that the body is a compilation of related interconnected parts. This sense of wholeness enables children to feel at home in their bodies and in turn allows children to explore the world of movement with confidence and competence (Sherborne 1990 p.111).

Griffiths and Cullingford (1990) consider that another advantage of relationship play is its ability to encourage children to use their body as apparatus.

> Far too little floor work is done in gym lessons. All too often its 'get the apparatus out'. Firstly children need to use the body as apparatus. In pairs or small groups children use the body to support, to obstruct, and to propel. The body can form a bridge, a tunnel, a box, a springboard (p.14).

Their evidence suggests that by the children using their bodies as apparatus through relationship play they can begin to learn to control and manage their bodies in time and space. Without this initial framework the quality of future apparatus work will be inferior (p.14). It seems evident therefore, that children need to learn how to control, manage and explore their bodies before they can learn how to handle apparatus and the challenging situations which the gymnasium can present. Relationship play presents a context in which the children can learn to control, manage and explore their own bodies and their partner's bodies before performing gymnastic and movement skills on conventional apparatus. For example, caring relationship activities encourage children to physically support their partner which may initially take the form of balancing on their partner's back and can progress onto more demanding activities which involve the transfer of weight from one body part to another; this can then be used to initiate vaulting or cartwheel moves.

Relationship activities also encourage children to support each other during gymnastic movements, a clear example of this is demonstrated when a child supports her partner in a headstand or a handstand. Paired learning experiences encourage the children to work co-operatively, supporting and caring for each other whilst learning about and performing gymnastic skills. Studies on relationship play (Mauldon and Layson 1979) have also revealed that it can enable children to experience gymnastic skills which are beyond their perceived ability;

...the most important factor and the reason for including this type of work in gymnastics is that in this situation activities can be explored and mastered (sic) which are impossible to do alone (p.169).

Their evidence indicates that through paired learning experiences children are able to perform, explore and accomplish gymnastic skills which cannot be experienced individually. My research has supported this view and Tim, a child from my case study, offers an example of this growth in confidence and ability. During the first few relationship play lessons Tim lacked movement confidence in gymnastics, however, with continual support and encouragement from his peers, he was able to slowly develop his self-assurance within gymnastics. Instead of performing safe and simple gymnastic movements whilst working with friends, Tim began to perform more demanding movement patterns which demonstrated quality, control and confidence.

Veronica Sherborne was significantly influenced in her thinking and teaching by Laban. His movement analysis (1969) was categorised into four aspects, that of time, weight, flow and space. By encouraging children to move in a variety of ways their understanding of movement is developed and enriched;

> ...the possibilities of the flow of the movement and the variety of rhythms brought about by the changing proportions of weight, space and time, enlarges and enriches the individuals capacity (Russell 1958 p.27).

Relationship play can provide children with opportunities to explore the complex world of movement, thus developing their movement vocabulary and also their understanding of the factors which influence the quality of the movement, such as body tension and clarity of body shape (DES 1991, p.33). Understanding and awareness of these factors means that children are able to make qualitative judgments about what they do or see, empowering children to become critical partners and to have greater autonomy and ownership of their work. However, the children need the necessary skills to manage and make sense of these experiences. This can be achieved through transferring control from the teacher to the child which consists of four strands: i) Doing; ii) Thinking and Talking; iii) Reflecting; and iv) Revisiting. [2]

For children to participate independently in the strands identified, it is imperative that the teacher gives the child the necessary tools to manage the experience (Dibbo and Gerry 1995). This involves helping the child to discover what to look for in her partner's movement and to provide words to appropriately describe her peer's performance. This could be described as a reflective process with the child as a 'reflective participant' where she evaluates and reflects on the task she has observed her partner doing and provides suitable feedback.

In the first few weeks of relationship play lessons the feedback the children gave to their partners was as simple as "Your forward roll was very tight". However, as the lessons progressed the children's ability to critically support their partner's developed in a more sophisticated manner. They began to comment on the qualitative aspects of their peers performance, such as "Your forward roll had continuity and flow". They also started to make constructive recommendations about how their partners could improve the quality of their performance, such as encouraging them to have a starting and finishing position. This in turn provided children with opportunities to refine and improve their skills by revisiting the tasks, thus developing their understanding of quality and control within gymnastics.

Evidence gathered from my research suggests that relationship play can contribute to children's development in the following areas; i) body awareness; ii) development of learning and performing of gymnastic skills; and iii) developing an understanding of movement and its qualities. However, through analysing the learning experiences provided to the children in

---

2 See John Dibbo, Chapter 3 of this book, for a more in depth discussion of this process.

the relationship play lessons, it became evident to me that the depth of development in these three areas is dependent upon the learning experiences in which the children engage. I suggest that there are a further two essential prerequisites to ensure effective learning takes place within relationship play activities.

1. The teacher must provide children with the appropriate skills and strategies to enable children to manage the learning experiences. This is described by Wood (1988) as contingent teaching; "By teaching children 'contingently' - that is, by making any help given conditional upon the child's understanding of previous levels of instruction..."(p.79) it involves the teacher structuring the tasks with progression and continuity, enabling the children to build on previous knowledge.

2. The teacher should also provide appropriate support to the learners as they engage in more complex tasks which is a constructivist teaching style (Watts and Bentley 1989 p.159).

   By helping the child to structure his activities, we are helping him (sic) to perform things he could not do alone until such time as he becomes familiar enough with the demands of the task at hand to develop local expertise and to try things alone (Wood 1988, p.77).

   This support may take the form of the teacher introducing tasks to the children which are relevant to their past experience or their prior knowledge. However, it may also take the form of the teacher adopting children's local expertise to enable them to manage the activity in hand at that time. According to Wood (1988) local expertise refers to the child learning about the task at hand (page 77). The notion of instructional scaffolding is similar as the teacher supports the learner through carefully structuring the learning experiences presented to the children.

Therefore, to ensure that the learning experiences and opportunities provided for the children enable them to develop gymnastic skills through relationship play I had to examine whether the teaching styles employed reflected the childrens' learning experiences. To work effectively with SDM the children have to be at the centre of the learning experience. For this reason a constructivist teaching style was adopted, including aspects of contingent, reciprocal (Mosston and Ashworth 1986, p.62) and instructional scaffolding teaching styles. By employing such an integrated teaching approach it enabled me to teach relationship play within an holistic framework which I argue, provides children with the necessary skills and knowledge to understand the whole experience. It also provided children with opportunities to explore the known and unknown world of movement, thus developing their movement vocabulary, their body awareness and gymnastic skills. As such, my research has revealed that relationship play can provide children with opportunities to develop gymnastic skills, dependent on whether the children are provided with the necessary tools (skill, knowledge, strategies and support) to enable them to manage the learning experiences and to have greater autonomy and ownership of their work (Dibbo and Gerry 1995). I suggest that relationship play can encourage children to manage the Physical Education experience and take responsibility for their own learning which encourages children to become independent learners by being involved in the continuous process of planning, performing and evaluating. By enabling children to have responsibility for their actions we are developing children's cognitive abilities to make decisions and be aware of the effects and consequences of their actions (DES 1992, p.3). Therefore, these experiences encourage children to engage not only physically, but cognitively, affectively and socially in a relationship play activity.

In conclusion, relationship play aims can enable children to explore the world of movement in a non-threatening environment, develop their self-confidence, their confidence in making and maintaining relationships and their understanding of movement itself. Skill acquisition in gymnastics follows on naturally from this initial framework and allows the individual to learn, perfect and perform a variety of movements. Sherborne and Laban both emphasised that developmental movement and relationship play aims;

> ...not so much to make successful performers as to develop the personality, to develop potential, and to help people to understand and experience the widest range of movement possible (Sherborne 1990 p.v).

This seems to me to be an appropriate aim for gymnastics teaching in the primary school.

References

DES (1991) National Curriculum Physical Education for ages 5 to 16 (Proposals) HMSO

DES (1992) Physical Education in the National Curriculum HMSO

Dibbo, J and Gerry, S (In press Spring 1995) "Physical Education Meeting the Needs of the Whole Child" in British Journal of Physical Education

Gallahue, D (1989) Understanding Motor Development - Infants, Children, Adolescents Benchmark Press 2nd Edition

Griffiths, B and Cullingford, S (1990) "What's in it for our kids? - Sherborne Movement, an Approach for all Pupils" The Bulletin of Physical Education Winter Vol 26. No. 3. pp 13-15

Laban, R (1960) L Ullman (Ed) Mastery of Movement 2nd Edition

Mace, R and Benn, B (1982) Gymnastic Skills Batsford Academic and Educational Limited

Mauldon, E and Layson, J (1979) Teaching Gymnastics Longman Group, 2nd Edition

Mosston, M and Ashworth, S (1986) Teaching Physical Education Merrill Publishing Company, 3rd Edition

Russell, J (1958) Modern Dance in Education MacDonald and Evans Limited

Sherborne, V (1990) Developmental Movement for Children Cambridge: Cambridge University Press

Watts, D and Bentley, M (1989) "Constructivism in the classroom: Enabling Conceptual change by Words and Deeds" in P Murphy and B Moon (Eds) Developments in Learning and Assessment The OU Press: Hodder and Stoughton

Woods, D (1988) How Children Think and Learn London: Falmer Press

Chapter 11

Movement as a means of communication

Leslie Craigie

Introduction

Within this paper there are two main points I would like to make:

i) To explain the history, background, theory and philosophy of Movement Therapy.

ii) To show how the work overlaps with much of Veronica Sherborne's teaching in content, theory and philosophy, if not in approach.

Movement Therapy (MT) has a relatively brief history in Scotland as 1986 saw the completion of the first MT course. This was an informal course, although it gained status with certification granted by Dunfermline College of Physical Education as a three year part-time course and trained seven students in the first cohort. Also in 1986, the Scottish Council for Movement Therapy (SCMT) was formed and ran another course which was not completed. At present the SCMT is unoperational with a view to reform in the future. August 1994 saw a draft proposal for a course entitled "An Introduction to Movement Therapy" submitted to Strathclyde University, Glasgow, as an initial step towards establishing a formally approved postgraduate MT course in Scotland. We acknowledge that Dance & MT courses at the Laban Centre, London and similar courses in other English colleges are established but point out that these courses have a different base and framework from therapy practised in Scotland. An appreciation of both approaches would be included in the proposed new course.

MT is best explained by becoming actively involved in movement communication activities and watching examples of these movement interactions of client and therapist caught on video. I describe the key points below indicating where the video material can be obtained which supports these points.

1. MT is appropriate for anyone with a block in communication including those with physical and/or mental disabilities, psychological or emotional problems, those suffering from post-trauma symptoms eg. ear accident and is also for depressed and stressed people.

2. MT is an alternative way to communicate using movement as language tools which include whole body actions as well as body parts moving, gestures and facial expressions.

3. MT is about being allowed into someone else's world where a relationship can be formed through the medium of movement. Consequently, it is about trust. Feelings about being secure are explored in actions that bring the client and therapist close together. When actual physical contact is involved, as in weight bearing activities, a great deal of trust is demanded. Rolling, swinging, lifting, lowering and sliding are examples of shared movements and link directly with Sherborne Developmental Movement (SDM).

4. MT is client-led where the control is given over to the client by the therapist.

5. MT uses the Mother-Infant interactive model. It is the style of the interaction between mother and young baby which forms the framework for communication and language in later years. The baby automatically produces certain facial expressions, gestures, body movements and vocalisations which are 'the mother's most crucial tools to regulate her half of the interaction with the infant' (Stern 1977). The therapist can work in a similar way with clients who have physical and/or learning difficulties.

Colwyn Trevarthen in his research at Edinburgh University has made studies of mothers and their 4-6 week old infants and noted the strong communications that carry on between them. He believes that the ability to communicate 'must be formulated largely within the brain before birth without benefit of imitation or training' (1974a). When the baby 'appears to copy the mother's actions', Trevarthen maintains that it 'is certainly not a passive incorporation of new experiences, it is more a re-modelling and integration of components already in spontaneous expression' (Trevarthen 1974b). A similar style of communication can develop between profoundly handicapped young people and their carers if their non-verbal conversations are 'built up slowly and consistently with an adult who has a perceptive, flexible and adaptable approach similar to the approach used by caregivers and their babies' (Burford 1986).

Evidence of these types of communications is found on a video made by Bronwen Burford[1]. It shows young adults interacting with their staff where the staff have been asked to imitate and fit in with the young person's movements. The staff use appropriate improvisational skills to allow client-led communication to flow. The staff are not trained MTs but know their clients well.

Further evidence of this type of work is captured on video by Judy Watson[2] at Gogarburn Hospital, Edinburgh. The movement interactions, also based on the mother-infant model, show turn-taking and synchronous movement interactions between children with severe learning difficulties and hospital staff. Again, the staff have no formal MT training but establish trusting relationships with the children through movement communication.

6. MT is concerned with looking for ways to connect with another person. One important connecting strand is using a similar style of movement which immediately makes the therapist accessible to her client. The therapist's job is to try to fit into the same way her client is moving. Rudolf Laban's Movement Factor Table of Weight, Time, Space and Flow provides a basis for the analytical process to identify the child's movement style and the therapist's movement preferences. It is important for the therapist to try to become as versatile in movement as possible. MTs also employed also included Laban's Movement Factors of for example, strong, light, fast, slow, direct, flexible, bound flow and free flow in her work as does SDM. Exploring these movement qualities helps the client to develop body awareness. It was by working in this way that Sherborne believed children, and of course adults too, would 'learn to use and control their bodies in many different ways and acquire a balanced movement vocabulary' (1990a). MTs, like Sherborne, recognise the importance of feeling 'at home' in their own bodies (1990b). Well developed body awareness fosters feelings of self-confidence and increased self-esteem which in turn allows movement language to flow more easily between two people.

---

[1] Video available from The Health Promotion Research Trust, 49-53 Regent Street, Cambridge CB2 1AB

[2] Video available from Moray House College of Education, Holyrood Campus, Edinburgh

7. Non-verbal communication concentrates on the expressive and creative side of movement rather than on the functional side of motor development.

> Skill development is not the Drama or Movement Therapist's primary aim... We must continue to maintain that our strength is that we focus on the creativity and on the quality of interactions rather than on the development of specific skills... It is a fundamental principle in the practice of Drama and MT that if the creative impulse is freed, the skills will develop alongside (Dawson 1994).

8. Improvisation skills are part of this work. Although we imitate the client in a turn-taking or synchronous way, we also improvise by using the movement factors to exaggerate, reduce or re-form the movements which are acceptable to the client.

> I have worked with a 7 year old autistic boy (Michael) engaging in lively, vigorous movement sequences. I often had to wait considerable periods of time before being allowed into his world. After the waiting period I was often rewarded with Michael wanting to connect with me - through sound or movement interactions or involving physical contact. It was my task to fit in and play with what he offered. Swings, rolls and activities where I accepted his body weight were skilfully initiated by this often unapproachable young boy. Many of the movements would also belong in SDM.

9. Although we are involved with the movement side of communication, it is difficult to ignore and be separate from the associated vocalisations. There are 'obvious and important similarities between language and bodily communication' (Birdwhistell 1970). Birdwhistell supported the idea that body, facial and head kinemes are vital parts of movement communication and should be placed within a verbal context. He did not accept the verbal and non-verbal dichotomy as valid. MTs share this view and use movements to answer certain sounds emitted by the client and use sounds to provide movement responses. By improvising with movement factors communication can be very powerful.

10. Stillness is an important part of the MT process. It accentuates the fact that control rests with the client. The piece of movement following a still period is most significant as it becomes highlighted by its position within the interactive sequence and is often very meaningful.

11. Meaningful connections between therapist and client need not involve large movements. Tiny, seemingly trivial throwaway actions may contain important messages for the therapist. It is surely important to accept whatever the child brings to the session, no matter how small that response is as 'at times, they may help us to find the lost key to still invisible doors...I always assume that the patient has no other way of telling me his story than the one he actually uses' (Millar 1987).

I conclude that MT is an appropriate type of intervention for people with severe communication difficulties because it is body based (paying attention to vocal communications as well) and also serves to promote relationship building and trust. SDM focuses on developing body awareness and concentrates on caring, relationship building activities. I see a principal difference in that SDM relies on a more direct approach while for the MT the client is the initiator and controller. Nevertheless, the two methods have distinct overlaps. The philosophy of MT does not fit in easily with the structured pedagogy of the National Guidelines for Expressive Arts in Scotland and England. However, because of its links with SDM it may well carve a place for itself in the National Guidelines for Curriculum and Assessment and support more effectively those children with Special Educational Needs.

References

Birdwhistell, R (1970) in M Argyle (Ed) Bodily Communication London: Methuen

Burford, H (1986) "Communication through Movement" in E Shanley (Ed) Mental Handicap : a Handbook of Care Edinburgh: Churchill Livingstone

Cheseldine, S (1991) "Gentle Teaching for Challenging Behaviour" in J Watson (Ed) Innovatory Practice and Sever Learning Difficulties Edinburgh: Moray House

Dawson, A (1994) "Drama therapy and Movement Therapy in Special Education" in Journal of the British Association for Drama therapists Vol 16 no.1

Hewett, D and Hind, M (1989) "Developing an Interactive Curriculum for Pupils with Severe and Complex Learning Difficulties" in B Smith (Ed) Interactive Approaches Birmingham: Westhill College

Miller, A (1987) The Drama of Being a Child London: Virago Press

Schaffer, R (1977) Mothering London: Fontana Press

Sherborne, V (1979) "Movement and Physical Education." in G Upton (Ed) Physical and Creative Activities for the Mentally Handicapped Cambridge: Cambridge University Press

Sherborne, V (1990) Developmental Movement for Children Cambridge: Cambridge University Press

Stern, D (1977) The First Relationship: Infant and Mother London: Open Books

Trevarthen, C (1979) "Communication and Cooperation in Early Infancy: A Description of Primary Intersubjectivity" in M Bullowa (Ed) Before Speech Cambridge: Cambridge University Press.

Chapter 12

Drama and Sherborne Teaching

Irene Rankin

... all children have two basic needs: they need to feel at home in their own bodies and so to gain body mastery, and they need to be able to form relationships (Sherborne 1990 p.v).

I first saw Veronica Sherborne in the film `In Touch', working with drama students, and it was this idea of introducing imaginative play within the sessions that encouraged me to take this further. I believe the inclusion of Sherborne Developmental Movement (SDM) within a drama context can add another dimension to drama. It can help the child who has learning difficulties to internalise and reflect on meaning thereby moving the experience on from mere enjoyment to expectations of the future. The use of language and group interaction as part of the experience can encourage feelings of cooperation and the achievement of a goal. The drama therapist, Sue Jennings (1981), has stated:-

Building relationships through movement is an important starting point in order to be able to proceed to more developed work as a means of expressing and sharing feelings. ...it is easy to forget when a child is severely damaged and may not be able to verbalise that he or she still has feelings to express... However severe the disability, we must remember the strength of feelings.

There is often a reluctance to deal with emotion in the classroom, for example it is as important for the leader to feel as confident and happy in a situation as the children. In the drama approach I recommend, (see appendix l), there are three strands which should help to make the learning process a 'safe' one:

1) There is a strong story line which helps the adults to communicate their feelings and emotions to the group. This story line should also mean something to the children, allowing them to become involved and eager to participate physically and mentally.

2) The sequencing and repetition of events introduces tension without which there is no drama.

3) Reflection upon the events allowing an outward expression of the kind of learning which has occurred.

Fantasy removes the thoughts from the classroom and it applies equally to the adults and the children! Indeed;

The relaxation generated by fantasy is likely to provide a means to bypass blocks to creativity. This same unblocking process may play an important part in Physical Education. Many Physical Education teachers complain that mental attitude is often a block to physical performance and fantasy may provide a methodology to release some of the blocks. Fantasy has been seen by some athletes and their trainers as a way to hone up skills and specific techniques and improve performance (Hall, Hall & Leech 1990).

This use of the imagination and projection into roles can motivate an inner learning which may not be immediately obvious to the observer. For example, during the playback to parents of a video showing a class taking part in rolling, a father suddenly realised what his multiply handicapped son had been trying to tell him to do when he kept pulling him down towards the floor. He wished to roll his father as he had been rolling an adult in school. The teachers knew he enjoyed the activity but they did not know he wished to transfer it to his home situation. Another child who never spoke about what happened at school jumped out of bed three times to relate to his family what had happened during the drama lesson.

I have followed Dorothy Heathcote's (1981) advice on the kind of fantasy and imaginative role play which I use incorporating movement experiences inspired by Sherborne.

> I never ask them consciously to pretend. To keep this reality I try to make something happen to which they only have to respond. These occurrences must really happen, for example a person may be there to meet them. A thing needing to be done might be there plainly demonstrating what needs doing. A combination of both may be there and the occurrence or person must be very clearly defined. For example, one of the methods I use often is to create a bizarre or noticeable provocation so that no one can miss it. It can intrude on their vision or their space. It is a gentle invasion, inexorable nevertheless and capable of constant development. To achieve this I tend to look to 'epic' materials for my provocations. Epic material bypasses 'little jobs' and reaches first for relationships out of which working together can begin. The basis of epic material lies in these areas: striving, feeling, great fearing, joy, labour, painful trials, carrying heavy responsibility or celebrating.

In other words, the elements of Drama!

The teacher should know the needs of the children which then determine the type of role and challenges offered. The challenge might be a physical one, such as those demanded using SDM. Unlike the actor, these roles are not performed for the benefit of an audience but for the satisfaction of the group and what can be learnt from the experience. These internal feelings cannot be obviously assessed by an observer. As stated before, however, the teacher/leader/carer is observing the involvement, commitment and reaction of each group member. Assessment of the experience is vital to determine what happens to the child during and after the experience.

Progression for me lies in important signs and facts;

1   the children or adults increasingly anticipate the presence of the 'role' or event;
2   they reflect on the event, their part in it afterwards and between meetings;
3   they take power over or within the events;
4   they show opinion and stick to it, thinking around it more and more;
5   there is a language flow and expression demonstrated which break into new language patterns or a change in physical demeanour; and
6   concentration begins to show intensity but also openness to others (Heathcote 1981).

If the child can internalise, reflect and report in an understandable way about their involvement in a drama experience then the records made by the teacher are invaluable to support and enhance the development and learning of that child. However, the assessments made are often based on non-verbal queues or signals or are reported by others. These reports might be vague and anecdotal but all should be recorded. Some findings will be subjective but still valid because, for example, I have acted. I have taken on the role of a character in a play.

I have understood the motivation behind a person wanting to do a certain action. I have not **been** that person, but acted **as if** I were that person, and hoped to represent the feelings and/or emotions that made the action take place. The important words here are **as if**. Sherborne has stated that children enjoy the exercises described as `Parcels' and `Prisons'. Perhaps this is because they can visualise a parcel. They know what a prison is. They therefore can act **as if** they **are** a parcel or **are in** a prison. Two children were observed by me mixing up some muddy water in a bowl and they invited me to see what was in it.

> "Mud and dead wasps!" they said with glee.
> "We're going to feed it to our prisoners!"

Like any good drama teacher, I felt privileged to be shown their magic drink and wanted to show I understood their actions.

> "And why have you captured the prisoners?"
> With a pathetic look directed at me, one child replied,
> "It's only play."

However, if the adult initiates a suitable context, serious and with obvious commitment, children will join in the 'make believe'. It is not `pretend' but is the same as the actor in the 'as if' situation. It is the leader's duty to present and create roles into which children can easily escape.

It must be remembered, however, that children with learning difficulties must be reminded at times that the drama is NOT for real. Stopping the drama and reflecting on and talking about what they are doing is one way to keep an objective approach. The specific moment when the drama stops must be clearly defined. Indeed, the children may have to be reminded they are not now in role and are back in the world of the classroom. This experiential learning method fits well into the Scottish Curriculum Guidelines (see appendix 2).

I use drama in this instance as a learning tool, an expression which often angers drama teachers. Learning experience is perhaps a happier term but no matter the terminology, in the field of Special Educational Needs, drama can present the opportunity to explore other worlds, meet challenges and make decisions in a safe environment and gain satisfaction from that experience. Satisfaction can encourage an inner self-esteem which should, in time, positively affect relationships with others.

Quest for the Sun (see appendix 1) was a valuable project for many reasons. The opportunity was given for the whole school, pupils and adults, to join together for a common purpose, encouraging the necessity for co-operation with others. The children were also encouraged, through the story-line, to show concern for each other which at the beginning of the project was not evident. They very quickly began to be aware of situations where help for others was needed and reacted accordingly. Pupils who had previously lacked the confidence to participate in role-play became enthusiastically involved; imaginations were also stimulated. The exploration of different ways of using parts of the body generated awareness of themselves. "The atmosphere for everyone throughout the theme was of total enjoyment, both for staff and pupils." (Teacher's Evaluation, Drummore School)

This combination of movement and drama brings together a wide range of experiences, both external and internal, and I will take the liberty of adding one word to Veronica Sherborne's (1981) quote:

> The movement (drama) lesson should be enjoyed by the teacher and helpers as much as by the children. The teacher ensures that all the children are successful and develops their potential as fully as possible.

References

Hall, Hall & Leech (1990) Scripted Fantasy in the Classroom   Routledge

Heathcote, D (1981) Drama & the Mentally Handicapped - The Arts & Disabilities MacDonald

Jennings, S (1981) Drama Therapy with Multi-handicap - The Arts & Disabilities MacDonald

Sherborne, V (1981) A Sense of Movement - The Arts & Disabilities MacDonald

Sherborne, V (1990) Developmental Movement for Children CUP

Appendix 1

The Quest for the Sun - (An Integrated Project)

AIM   to involve the children in a project where they will experience music, movement, art and language, bound together within a drama context.

Before the children begin this project they must have experience and confidence in the SDM. It is therefore essential that movement as pure exercise precedes the project work. Older children can help the younger and less able children, but the project should encourage change of role and responsibility. The ideas are outlined, but the teachers and children should feel free within the wide story-line to change the suggested challenges, movement, language and music.

The specific needs of the children should be examined. We wish the group to not only enjoy their participation, but to be challenged and stretched. This might mean a movement challenge, an interaction challenge, a concentration challenge, a confidence challenge. These decisions are left to each leader or teacher as they know the needs of the individuals and the group. At the completion of the project, the leader/teacher should be able to look at the record of involvement of each child and to note where success and/or failure lay. This can give guidelines for further progress.

Although the project may end with parents and friends seeing the story of `The Quest For The Sun', it must be remembered that it is the work, experimentation and acceptance of challenge which really counts. The process is of great importance although great satisfaction can be gained from the pride of showing what `I can do' to others. In fact to date, each group has wished to keep the experience to themselves, although parents have heard a great deal about the story at home.

The Story - The Quest for the Sun
Part 1
Once upon a time there was a land far away.
The people were very unhappy.
The rain rained every day, and the sun never shone.

The leader called his people to him.
"Dear people! Our country needs the sun.
I have heard that if you go on a long and tiring journey, you can bring back some rays of sun which will bring heat and bright light.
Are you prepared to go, and search for the Sun?
So the people set off.

But as soon as they left their land, they found the road blocked by large and heavy rocks. They heard a voice say, "Push, push! Use your strength and the rocks will move! They thought really hard and prepared themselves to push. Some people needed to help others, but finally the rocks were pushed aside, and they rested, because they knew they still had a long way to go.

Part 2
The next day they went on their way, but not too far along the road they found star fish stretched out, blocking their way.
They heard a voice say, "Step carefully over the stinging star fish. Do not touch them! Step carefully and you will be safe."
So carefully, and helping each other, they stepped over the starfish, and then they rested after that adventure.

Part 3
And then they saw the sun shining above them.
They heard a voice say, "Climb up and ask the Sun to give you some of the rays. If you are asked, you can explain why you need them."
So they climbed up and persuaded the sun to give them each a sun ray. Then they thanked the Sun, and rested before the journey home.

Part 4
They set off carrying their sun rays but they lost their way! "Tell us how to get home!" they shouted.
They heard the voice say, "Do not worry. Look, and you will see a tunnel, through which you will have to crawl."
So they crawled through the long tunnel, one by one.

But their troubles were not yet over.
A long monster lay on the road in front of them.
"Do not worry!" said the voice. "This is a kind and sleeping monster. Crawl along its back. At the end of the road your leader is waiting!" So they crawled along the back of the creature, and all together safely reached their leader and their home.

"Well Done, my people!. Let us put your sun rays together. Feel the heat and see the light. Our land will be happy again!"

And they celebrated the coming of the Sun to their land and told the story of their journey many, many times.

The Process : a) Elements

1 P.E/Movement :	The exercises MUST be experienced first at a discrete level.	
	This will take time and may change the suggested format which follows.	
2 Drama :	Drama introduces the story and tension into the activity. The other areas should follow naturally and where appropriate.	
	`The Quest' can be broken into parts enabling the participants to focus on one type of challenge. Therefore the guidance given for the structured series of sessions which follow is only a suggestion and must be changed and adapted to suit the needs of the group.	
3 Language :	**Sound** could be introduced first of all and this might and could link up with **music.**	
	What vocal sound might the star fish make?	
	Is there a spell we have to chant and/or sing as we climb to fetch the sun's rays?	
	Can one child be a story teller?	

	Can one adopt the role of the leader of the country? Can one adopt the role of the sun, reluctant to give up the rays?

4 Music : Separate creative music workshops are needed to allow experimentation. Perhaps there might be music to portray the MOOD of the opening. Perhaps a star fish "motif". The footsteps could be echoed on a different musical instrument. Perhaps a sun "motif". The movement of climbing **upwards** could be depicted instrumentally A creature "motif", also with much in the way of **action** music! Perhaps there might be music to portray the **mood** of the closing scene.

5 Art : As with Music, within workshops, differing tasks can be carried out. Help the children to think like an artist, i.e. take source material from books and develop it through various techniques. Cut a paper sun, using folding and cutting techniques. Create suns, using dribbled paint, emphasising colours and how they mix. Design a "motif" for a tee shirt. Screen paint the above. Make sun rays or beams in different ways.

6 Reflection & Evaluation: After every session related to `The Quest' discussion should take place, where children can relate their experiences.

My thanks are due to June McGregor, Music Lecturer, St Andrew's College, and Val Hamilton, visiting Art Teacher, Drummore School, Oban, for their help in the areas of Music and Art.

The Process : b) The programme - some guidelines
The Sherborne Movement exercises **must** be introduced to the children before beginning this kind of Drama approach. They may be more used to working with P.E. apparatus rather than with the physical contact with other people, and this may prove to be strange and difficult at first. Once the group are confident with the skills in relationship play, simple drama ideas can be introduced. e.g. Walking on the moon, a journey through a jungle, scenarios which can utilise the movement skills previously experienced and enjoyed.

The method of introducing `The Quest' is important. The children must realise they are going to be working on something important, and there should be a feeling of ritual each time the `Quest' sessions are started. This can be encouraged by moving to a different space, dimming the lights and/or playing a music theme. Every time `The Quest' is acted out, it will be different. I cannot predetermine the outcome. All I can give is a possible, not probable outline.

1 Tell the whole story...
Not every child will remember it, but an awareness of the whole feeling of an epic story should be apparent from the beginning. This is as much for the teller and leader of the sessions as the participants. Invite the children to accept the challenge of the journey. If you have invested a great deal of atmosphere into the story telling, they should be eager to take up the challenge! Act out Part One, focussing on the feeling of strength and perhaps cooperation involved. While resting, reflect on the first task, and how well they performed it. Can any one remember what they will meet next?

You may wish to create music at this point for Part One, or leave it till later.

2 The star fish...
Create excitement at the thought of continuing the acting-out of the story. You might want to repeat part One, adding on the new movement focus after a short rest, or if the children can recount the first part of the adventure, you can start the acting-out with the encounter with the star fish. How you do this is up to you, for example with a large group some can be the star fish.

Older children, formally recruited, and given the importance of their task can adopt the roles which challenge the travellers. This can be a different kind of challenge for an older group, and can foster the ideas of caring and taking on responsibility. Try and bring **sound** into this session. Each session should end with a rest and reflection time. Consider : i) How much time do you wish to devote to `The Quest'? and ii) How much reinforcement do you wish to build in, without letting the children become bored with the journey?

3 Art work might start to run alongside...
Remember, the Art is not merely supplying the props for the story. New skills can be achieved, new understandings gained, and joy will be experienced when the skills link up within the drama context, becoming one whole artistic endeavour.

4 How do we get the suns rays?
This might be a problem solving activity, with the teacher-in-role as the Sun, reluctant to give up some rays.

5 The return journey...
You may not want to do Part Four in one session. This will depend on your on-going assessment of the children's commitment and involvement. It will also depend on the make-up of the group, and whether the participants can adopt different roles. You may also be building in music and other ideas which have come from the group's reflections on the journey.

Appendix 2

The curriculum 5 - 14 Scottish Education Department
Principles governing the curriculum 5 - 14

Breadth;   provides appropriate experiences to ensure the coverage of a sufficiently comprehensive range of areas of learning;
Balance;   ensures that appropriate time is allocated to each area of curricular activity and that provision is made for a variety of learning experiences;
Coherence;   requires the establishment of links across the various areas of learning so that pupils begin to make connections between one area of knowledge and skills and another;
Continuity;   ensures that learning builds on pupils' previous experience and attainment;
Progression;   provides pupils with a series of challenging but attainable goals.

Appendix 3 - The Expressive Arts Curriculum

Aims: The expressive arts should provide all pupils with opportunities:

to promote pupils' affective development
to promote pupils' physical development
to contribute to pupils' personal development
to contribute to pupils' social development
to promote an awareness of cultural heritage, values and diversity

Drama

Aims 5-14: _Drama should provide all pupils with opportunities:

to reach new understandings and appreciation of self others and the environment through imaginative dramatic experience to communicate ideas and feelings through language, expression and movement, in real and imaginary contexts

to develop confidence and self esteem in their day-to-day interaction with others

to develop sensitivity towards the feelings, opinions and values of others through purposeful interaction

to develop a range of dramatic skills and techniques

Why Drama?

`...all children have two basic needs: they need to feel at home in their own bodies, and so to gain body mastery, and they need to be able to form relationships.'
(Veronica Sherborne 1990)

The drama context can provide children with the relationships they need, which can be with oneself, with peer groups and with the outside world. They also need an understanding of relationships in other contexts, again this can be provided through the drama experience by using, for example, elements of our literature, history or aspects of religious education.

Chapter 13

Sherborne Development Movement
and
Language Development

Kathryn Firth and Linda Sired

Introduction

We started our project from a basic philosophical perspective that locates children at the centre of the learning process within a framework of essential equality where;

> All children have the right to an education appropriate to their motor, cognitive and affective level of development (Gallahue, 1993 p.9).

The project began in Spring 1993 at a First School with the first practical movement session held in April 1993. A small group of third year BEd undergraduates specialising in primary Physical Education were the research team and we present this paper as part of that work. The school involved has an assessment unit and a language unit with special education facilities provided for children with a variety special needs. The children have specialist teachers but are fully integrated into all mainstream activities allowing them complete access to the National Curriculum. Physiotherapists from a special school in Devon had also been involved in a clinical context with some of the children for a long period of time.

A joint programme approach was organised to utilise this collective expertise in a multi-disciplinary approach. The referral of children taking part in the programme was the responsibility of the class teachers who had observed how the children reacted in the classroom situation. The movement group was a mixed group consisting of 12-15 children of 5-8 years old from the assessment unit, the language unit and mainstream schools. The four children for this case study came from the language unit (See appendix 1 for details on each individual child). Each child was assessed by physiotherapists individually using the assessment profile developed by Henderson and Sugden (1992) "Movement Assessment Battery For Children". This assessment enables identification of the strengths and problems the child experiences in a movement situation.

Each practical session lasted for 1 hour and had 3 elements (see appendix 2):

1. **Sherborne Developmental Movement (SDM)** - with the intention of developing locomotor and stability skills as well as relationship work within the group and project team;

2. **Individual work** - focussing on manipulative movements of a gross and fine nature; and

3. **Parachute games** - which included locomotor, manipulative and stability movement skills. This reinforced the social skills of active listening and turn-taking in interactive situations.

Design and procedure of study

The main research focus was on the relationship between and the development of language and movement. The analysis of the findings explored the impact of language and movement on how children think and learn. However, for us as teachers, it was important to manage the affective dimension for ourselves and the children with such individual needs. We used carefully structured group building activities to achieve this additional aim. The objectives for the main research project were;

i) to develop teaching strategies to enhance the development of children with identified movement difficulty from a multi-disciplinary perspective; and

ii) to address the learning needs of the whole child through different approaches to Physical Education.

Method

The four boys attended SDM sessions for one hour on Wednesday afternoons. These sessions included 10-12 children from the assessment/diagnostic, language and mainstream units. For six half hour sessions we worked with the children on their identified language problems using movement to aid exploration. The hall was made into a simple obstacle course using ropes, balls, cones, hoops, mats etc. We gave the boys various sequences of instructions which they then had to physically perform and asked them to recall their movements and give instructions to each other. These sessions reinforced movement skills concentrating on the language skills of sequencing, understanding and giving instructions, using present and past tense and the use of sentences including the words 'before' and 'after'. Every Thursday afternoon, for approximately 45 minutes, the four boys attended a language and speech therapy session where teaching was directed towards their individual language difficulties including word/picture games, written exercises, discussions and picture sequencing.

Case study

Choosing a case study approach enabled us to examine how these children learnt. We hoped to establish links between language and movement for children who have language difficulties and thus produce a suitable programme to develop not only the physical aspect of the child but to try to meet the needs of the whole child.

> ...an important criterion for judging the merit of a case study is the extent to which the details are sufficient and appropriate for the teacher working in similar situations to relate his decision making to that described in the case study. The relatability of a case study is more important than its generalability (Bassey, 1981, p.85).

Gallahue and McClenagan's (1978) "Fundamental Movement Pattern Assessment Instrument" was used for observation purposes. Various types of data collection were used; a video was made of the early sessions of the main project and of the six sessions using the obstacle and language movement lessons; still pictures were taken of various skills during the movement and language sessions; and taped interviews where the children were asked questions about the movement sessions (Appendix 4). A concern of the research was to understand the child's perception of his environment, seeking insight rather than statistical analysis.

> ...sometimes it is only by taking a practical instance that we can obtain a full picture of the interaction (Nisbet and Watt 1980, p.5).

The main project has been monitored by three main methods as suggested by Bell (1987) to provide a three dimensional picture which 'will illustrate relationships, micro-political issues and patterns of influences in a particular context' (p.7).

1. The teachers observed changes and identified improvements in some aspects in the presentations of their children. Individual files have been and are still being collected for this assessment.

2. Individual parental files were collected to help develop effective communication pathways about the progress of the children.

3. An objective view of the developmental progress of each child was made by testing them on the Henderson/Sugden assessment profile.

Conclusions

We believe that whilst experiencing an action and saying the 'action' word (eg: learning to catch and bounce a ball, repeating verbally "drop and catch") develops the child's understanding of language and his movement experience. For example, the boys' movements became more organised and coordinated using 'language for rhythm' whilst 'doing' the movement and associating the action with the word. Glasersfeld (1989) discusses this idea and believes that in order to attach meaning to a word a child must isolate it within their experiential world and acquire the ability to visualise/imagine the word with that experience. He further states that children must experience language and movement until they become aware of the 'neatness of fit' that can exist.

Our observations of the children in this research project support this idea that children develop a better understanding of the concept of movement through language and that the use of language is reinforced through positive movement experience. Speech is a physical activity and a way of controlling one's body in order to achieve goals and avoid discomfort (Vygotsky 1962). This physical activity also becomes internalised to create verbal thinking. Language and movement are interlinked, they rely upon each other for development and have a continual circular relationship and are critical to the 'whole being'. They help the individual interpret the world and make sense of experiences.

However, individuals develop at different rates and times so we should take care about setting artificially normative standards when considering a child's progress. Learning is active not passive and thus through the process of developing language and movement skills concurrently these children were given a clear way of understanding abstract concepts. A multi-disciplinary approach is important for these youngsters as it gives continuity through the learning processes by reinforcing their understanding of the relationship between language and movement. For example, problem solving and questioning have been found to be useful teaching methods so that the children can work at their own pace and level of development.

Guidance takes the form of either questions or changes in the experiential field that may lead the child into situations where his present way of operating runs into obstacles and contradictions. The child is unlikely to modify a conceptual structure unless there is an experience of failure or surprise at something not working out in the expected fashion (Glasersfeld 1989). The child must feel good about himself so he feels less inhibited about his difficulties. For the children in this project we believe that their self confidence developed greatly and evidence gathered through further visits show they now volunteer for tasks and express themselves more effectively than before.

Finally, if we accept that the cognitive, affective and motor development dimensions are interrelated (Gallahue 1989), then the problems of development cannot be addressed in isolation. Therefore, Physical Education does not serve the physical alone, we cannot teach in seclusion as this will deny the other important dimensions for the children. Whilst the research project has focussed on the relationship between language and movement we acknowledge the embodied relationship between the cognitive, physical and affective factors as they are integrated and not compartmentalised (Whitehead 1988).

References

BAALPE (1989) Physical Education for Children with Special Educational Needs in Mainstream Education White Press

Bee, H (1992) The Developing Child Harper Collins College Press

Bell, J (1987) Doing your own Research Project Open University Press

Cohen, L and Manion, L (1989) Research Methods in Education Routledge

Gallahue, D (1993) Developmental Physical Education for Today's Children Benchmark Press

Gallahue, D (1989) Understanding Motor Development: Infants, Children, Adolescents Benchmark Press

Murphy, P and Moon, B (1989) Development in Learning and Assessment Open University Press, Hodder and Stoughton

Reid, A (1990) Autism - A World Apart Culverts Press

Russell, J (1988) Graded Activities for Children With Motor Difficulties Cambridge University Press

Sherborne, V (1990) Developmental Movement for Children, Mainstream, Special Needs and Pre-school Cambridge University Press

Sherborne, V (1990) "Partner work" in British Journal of Physical Education Winter

Sparkes, A (1992) Research in Physical Education and Sport: Exploring Alternative Visions Falmer Press

Stenhouse, D (1975) An Introduction to Curriculum Research and Development Heinneman Press

Sugden, D and Keogh, J (1990) Problems in Movement Skill Development University of South Carolina Press

Sugden, D (1989) Cognitive Approaches in Special Education The Falmer Press

Whitehead, M (1988) "Dualism, Monism and Health Related Exercise in PE" in British Journal of Physical Education Newsletter 19

Whitehead, M and Capel, S (1993) "Teaching Strategies and Physical Education in the National Curriculum in British Journal of Physical Education Winter

Wood, D (1988) How Children Think and Learn Blackwell Press

Case studies were compiled on four six year old boys from the language unit with information being gained from a variety of sources eg: physiotherapists, teachers etc.

A 7 years old in May 1994. He came to the school with a statement of language disorder. He comes from a loving family. He has comprehension and expressive language breakdown. His language is disordered and has a development delay of 6-8 months. His vocabulary and grammar knowledge is two years behind his actual age. His understanding of vocabulary used by others is low. so he has difficulty understanding instructions. He dribbles constantly and this is believed to be due to lack of oral awareness. His speech therapist believes that his short term memory store may be problematic. This child shows clumsy symptoms and needs strong direction. He is socially unaware and uses inappropriate behaviour. He has co-ordination problems especially in fine-motor skills.

B 7 years old. This child had a difficult birth, he suffered lack of oxygen resulting in Anoxia and was born blue. He has suffered many food allergies over the years and lost a great deal of weight at an early age. He was diagnosed as having cerebral palsy in December 1989, his parents prepared for this but no symptoms ever presented themselves. He didn't walk until 18 months and had to be told to use his feet instead of crawling. This child came with a statement from an educational psychologist, a doctor and a speech therapist. His language problems appear to be genetic, with his younger sister also in the unit. His language expression and comprehension is only at 4 years and 2 months. His grammar is less than 3 years and 6 months, nearly half his actual age. His naming vocabulary is at 4 years. This child is bordering on autistic. He hates change and so needs a routine. His reading is good, but shows poor comprehension and has poor memory.

Both children attend a speech therapy lesson every Thursday afternoon. Boy A has been using past tense, 'before' and 'after' and looking at sequencing. Boy B is learning how to use connecting words, for example, 'because' and 'so'. He has been using pictures to sequence and order his language. Both boys are assessed every six months using the "Clinical Evaluation of Language, Fundamental Revised Test (CELFR).

L 7 years old. This child initially attended the Assessment and Diagnostic Unit, but due to his lack of understanding comprehension he was moved to the Language Unit. His is integrated into the mainstream part of the school every Thursday afternoon. He has regular sessions with the speech therapist who works with him on his grammatical language - past tense verbs, more complex sentences and sequencing . He has problems with understanding semantics and cannot process much aural information at a time due to a short term memory deficit. He has an occasional hearing loss and is clumsy in his actions. The size of his head as a younger child was very large in relation to his body although his body growth has now caught up. From the 'Movement Assessment Battery for Children (Henderson and Sugden 1990), the total impairment scores show that 'L' has a definite motor problem. His manual dexterity, ball skills and static and dynamic balance are all well below the norms for his age.

G 7 years old. He is in the Language Unit full time. He is integrated into mainstream every Thursday afternoon and again has two session with the speech therapist. He has both movement and verbal dyspraxia as a result of a very fast birth. He moves very quickly, mainly to keep his balance. When speaking, he stamps his foot and moves his head forward in his effort to speak due to his organic hemispheric problem. He has only recently been able to see in 3D since getting some new glasses. His reading, maths and spelling are good, although writing is a problem and his listening skills are poor. 'G's Total Impairment

Scores and checklist scores from the Movement ABC test also show that he has definite movement problems.

Appendix 2

Example of Movement Sessions - THEME - Shapes; over and under

Section 1 - Sherborne Developmental Movement

1. Moving in and out of each other, when drum is banged freeze in shape. (Use 'freeze', 'still', 'frozen' action words.)
2. Teachers make a shape (different levels), children explore the shapes. Different ways of travelling 'over' and 'under'.
3. Children make various shapes for the teachers to explore.
   [In points 2 and 3 teaching point is to ask the children to use the words 'over' and 'under' as they perform the movements]
4. Teachers make a long tunnel in a single line. Children explore the tunnel, travelling 'over' and 'under'.

Section 2 - Individual Work

1. Bead threading.
2. Spatial awareness puzzles.

Section 3 - Parachute Games

1. Shaking the parachute 'shake, shake, shake', changing speeds.
2. Climbing the mountain.
3. Cat and mouse.
4. Make a tent.

Appendix 4

Interview Questions

1. Can you remember how long you have been coming to the movement sessions?
2. What do you enjoy about the movement sessions? Why?
3. Are there things that you do not enjoy in the movement sessions? Why?
4. What do you like about working with the group?
5. Various questions about the photographs to see if the boys understand what is happening in the pictures.
6. What do you like best of all about your language sessions? Why?
7. What do you dislike about your language sessions? Why?
8. How and why do you think you have changed since coming to the movement and language sessions, if at all?

Chapter 14

Developmental Movement introduced in the National Curriculum of Special Education in Flanders

Willy Dewinter & Rita Vermeesch

In September 1992 Developmental Movement based on Veronica Sherborne's work was introduced in the Special Education system of the Flemish Federal Education Department (ARGO). Rita Vermeesch and Willy Dewinter, both working in special education and well experienced in Sherborne Developmental Movement (SDM), were asked by the appropriate authority to introduce SDM in primary and secondary schools for mentally and physically handicapped children. They accepted this challenge enthusiastically, and Walter Ven der Perren, a pedagogue connected to the training-centre 'Dialoog' was also asked to contribute because of his experience in this area.

Rita Vermeesch is a physiotherapist and teacher trainer for special education who has previously worked in a primary school, 'De Beverties' for mild and severe multiply handicapped young children (two and a half to thirteen years old) at Kasterlee, Antwerp. Willy Dewinter has a teaching degree in Dutch, English and Economics but is now connected to a secondary school 'De Mast' for mild and severe mentally handicapped youngsters (13-25 years) at Kasterlee, Antwerp.

An SDM course was organised by Rita and Willy and all the staff from special schools in the region have been trained over the last two years. A wide range of staff involved in special education attended these courses which included head teachers, teachers, physiotherapists, speech therapists, occupational therapists, ortho-pedagogues, educators from boarding-schools, nurses, trained children's nurses, head teachers of Psycho-Medical-Social-Centres and people from Central Administration, Brussels. In fact, whole school teams were instructed in order to create the opportunity to bring several people together from the same institution in one session, each with their own professional input, to work with the youngsters.

Sherborne Developmental Movement became a teachers course

On several occasions both authors attended workshops in Leuven organised by 'Dialoog', where Cindy and George Hill[1] gave movement sessions. From this starting point Willy was eager to organise sessions in his school. He talked about SDM to his colleagues and passed the information through to anyone who would listen. Unfortunately, at this early stage hardly anyone was interested. However, after a few years of intensive SDM he started adding rhythm and creative dance to his movement sessions. This decision was inspired by movement theatres working in schools in Belgium and as such influenced his teaching using SDM. This evolved and soon Willy developed his own Movement Theatre, called 'De -Blauwe Maan' (the Blue Moon). The actors themselves created the movement plays which were based on their own creativity during rehearsals. 'De Blauwe Maan' was quite a success and each time the performances in the famous "Warande Theatre" were sold out. However, the real success for Willy was that at last there was interest for what he and his colleagues were doing which then had a beneficial effect on his work in schools. That it had been possible to get youngsters

---

[1] Founder members of the UK Sherborne Federation and leading experts on SDM.

with special needs to be able to perform on stage for one hour when they were perceived in schools to have only a 2 minute concentration span was considered amazing. Colleagues were also impressed that the parents were a part of the process being involved in taking care of clothing, decorating and so on.

Rita did not need a theatre to get the attention in her school for SDM. She and some paramedic colleagues formed an enthusiastic team who saw the immediate value which the method could offer to their population of disabled children. After working from a rather cognitive base at first, the practical sessions more adapted to the needs of multiply handicapped children. On one of the trips Cindy Hill made to Belgium, all the teachers in the school were fortunate to have a one day-workshop from this marvellous teacher! As the team evolved as conductors, reflections on their experiences and feed back information from discussions brought them to review planning for their work with the multiply handicapped children. Gradually SDM became an important supporting element in their pedagogical approach.

Fortunately, the head teachers of their respective schools (Willy's and Rita's) were convinced of the success and joy SDM brought for the children. After both head teachers became members of the Inspection team for special education one of them, Ivo Pelckmans, made a request to the Federal Education Department to start a project on Veronica Sherborne Developmental Movement Teaching. As a result Rita and Willy were brought together to set up an SDM course.

The organisation of the course

The course consisted of a 2 days workshop, followed by regular work in the schools where every participant worked with their own group of children. The first day of the course started with a movement session followed by reflection about the framework of SDM (body, spatial awareness and building relationships). The approach and philosophy of Veronica Sherborne and the direct connection with the work of Rudolf Laban were presented to the course members. Throughout the course the links between theory and practice were constantly made. Reflection about the practical experience delivered on the course and discussion about the adaptability of SDM to each group of youngsters, their different handicaps, group leading styles and the children being part of the-group at their level of mental and physical ability, and so on, formed a key aspect of the course. This experiential work was supported in the afternoon with video material of youngsters experiencing SDM.

After a session of body awareness and building relationships the participants were asked to do some 'homework'. They were asked to try out SDM with their own group of children at their school. Subsequently, they returned and were asked to demonstrate the activities they experienced with their group in school.

The second day of the workshop began with a presentation of this 'homework'. Other course members acted as the children and afterwards there was discussion and reflection on the work. For example such questions as:- What were the obstacles you met in school? What were the reactions from the youngsters in your school? What were the reactions from the school team? This discussion was conducted in a positive and supportive atmosphere. The day continued with more activities about relationships followed by video analysis and discussion. In conclusion a movement session was organised about spatial awareness. The course members also received a syllabus with theoretical backing, practical activities and a bibliography to support their work in school.

At the end of the second day of the course appointments were made for a visit to the different schools by the course leaders (Willy and Rita) to observe the course members working with their class in school. Every school was visited four times to give as much time for discussion about SDM in schools and to maintain contact between Rita and Willy and the teachers in the participating schools.

At a later stage a one-day workshop was organised for the head teachers which included the main ideas from the two day course but in an abbreviated version. Deliberately Rita and Willy waited to organise this workshop until several teachers had been instructed. This strategy was designed to try to prevent uninterested head teachers from passing on their lack of interest to their staff. On this one day course the head teachers were informed by the project team how the course was structured so they could fit the project into their overall school plans.

Whenever participants of the workshops returned to their schools they talked a lot about what they had experienced either in a positive or a negative way. In fact, some responses were rather extreme. However, being active in a movement session melted away a lot of resistance and the great majority of teachers had good fun and had never met their colleagues in such a way. Very often there was a friendly, creative atmosphere.

People who had attended workshops in the first year, who had organised movement sessions in their own schools and wanted to know more about SDM, were invited to a one day follow-up workshop during their second year. This day focussed on observation, total communication, evaluation, introspection, problem solving, creativity, and deepening their philosophical understanding of SDM. Problem solving, where people tried to find solutions for specific problems experienced in movement sessions was, for a lot of participants very valuable. They felt that they received support not only from us, but also from each other. However, some colleagues only wanted ready made exercises rather than accompanying others on the track that leads to a deeper philosophical insight about SDM.

In some schools you can feel the positive atmosphere where affection and social-emotional development is rated at least as equally high as cognitive development. This change in attitude can only be achieved when the staff share a similar philosophy about movement. The fact that our youngsters enjoy movement sessions is often the motivation for the teachers to organise more sessions. We advise people who start organising movement sessions to make video recordings. This helps the teachers afterwards to evaluate their work and to assess the progress being made by the children.

Video material is available arising from the work of Willy De Winter and Rita Vermeesch filmed in three different schools in Flanders. It is an instructional video in three parts; i) 'Lichaamsaccoorden' (Body - chords) which looks at SDM with those who have mild and severe mental impairment; ii) 'Vlakbii' (Nearby) which shows SDM working with children who are autistic; and iii) 'Oei ik beweeg. Hoi. ik beweeg' (Ugh! I'm moving. Hurray, I'm moving) looking at SDM and children with multiple and complex disability. The video is used during the second year on the developmental programme in Flanders when staff are more experienced in the use of SDM. It shows the extent to which SDM can contribute to work with children with special needs. [2]

As with the staff, the head teachers are invited to a one day follow-up workshop which focusses on new developments learned from the implementation of current ideas using SDM in special schools. The involvement of these senior staff is critical as they are responsible for the strategic planning in their schools. Therefore, keeping them up to date with the work in this area helps to encourage these new initiatives and reduce any negative thinking.

There is generally felt in Belgium society that there has been a change of emphasis which now places more value on the socio-emotional development of the children through education. Thus, for example, the Government aims for the education of the less able children concentrates on providing them with more opportunity to feel emotionally safe in their surroundings. It is felt that this approach adds to the quality of education received and matches the underlying philosophy of SDM.

[2] The video is available for sale from The Pedagogical Centre for Special Education in Brussels.

As SDM and the work of the project team became established they received requests for workshops from groups not part of the original project plans. These groups included physiotherapy students, student gymnastic teachers, students in youth care and teachers' courses for special education. The success of the project can also be measured in the number of those participating in courses. In the first year 435 colleagues participated in the initial 2 day course with 280 colleagues being visited in their schools by the project team to see them teach. In the second year of the project this momentum was maintained with 434 colleagues taking the two day course, 211 being visited in schools and 286 attending the first 'one day' follow up course. Overall 38 special schools have been involved in the project so far.

Conclusion

Working with SDM at such an intensive level has changed us. In the beginning being positive was not always obvious and not always easy, but we feel we have grown as conductors. We have learnt not to blame people who bring up any reason for not attending courses. We have also seen the true complexity of human nature and have often admired our colleagues for their flexibility. It has been very satisfying for us to work with so many children in 38 schools all over Flanders. They have often moved us and we are proud to say that they all remember us.

Further, our work has made us more alert when it comes to standing up for weaker members of our society and made it easier for us to discover those who are most vulnerable. Working together as a team and giving each other support made us more effective in the delivery and development of Sherborne's ideas and philosophy. We were fortunate to establish the course as we saw fit without interference from the administration. We were allowed to take the initiative and to be as creative as possible. For the future, it is important that our colleagues are not left alone in the coming years, indeed they ask for regular contact and support. The same can be said for us, the Sherborne teachers, as the importance of International meetings cannot be denied. It is a great feeling to be members of the same International Sherborne Foundation Family.

Chapter 15

Sherborne Movement in a Specific Context

Janet Sparkes

This short paper (more aptly described as a case study) is based on an evaluation of the use of Developmental Movement (hereafter referred to as Sherborne Developmental Movement - SDM) with children 3 years to 8 years in a Romanian orphanage. SDM was part of a programme of stimulation which included the use of music and the visual arts. It is important to state that the environment from which the observations and subsequent analysis are made was not a 'clinical' setting; that is, it wasn't created with the intention of measuring the impact of certain experiences. The claims that are therefore made must be seen in this context and must be recognised as being the result of a somewhat subjective analysis of the situation.

The implementation of SDM in this environment was, for me, a very natural thing to do; there was an instinctive feel that it was exactly the kind of experience the children needed and from which they would benefit. But, was it only instinct? I think not! My analysis over a number of years of the SDM approach has left me in no doubt that this approach has its roots in sound developmental constructs. The approach, I would suggest, is not based on one particular conceptual model but draws on a number of models and theories all of which have a concern to understand the developing child as a physical, social, emotional and intellectual being - a coherent unit. The approach can also be characterised, I believe, by its concern for the process of learning - the experience of the child and adult (as it was in the orphanage setting) is central to the thinking of the educator. How the child learns matters equally to what the child learns.

For a moment I digress from the orphanage setting to make one further observation about the approach to working with children and adults as developed by Sherborne. One theory (as opposed to model) that I would suggest was influential in shaping Sherborne's approach was the theory of personality put forward by Carl Rogers in 1959. He viewed personality as something dynamic, with the potential to change. He argued that human beings have a basic need to 'develop their potential' as fully as possible. Problems develop when this is consistently denied. Rogers evolved his theory of personality by examining another basic need individuals have for 'positive regard', that is, the need for love, affection and respect. As will be noted later, these basic needs were consistently denied in the orphanage setting and an awareness of such was very influential in designing the kind of programmes that were implemented. Similar 'understandings' of personality to those expressed by Rogers can be found in Sherborne's writings.

This view of personality (scantily presented it must be recognised) is only one amongst several and the purpose of making reference to it here, in an uncritical fashion, is to stimulate some thought about the thinking underlying SDM for children.

The recipients of the programme ... the children.

The group of orphans, classified, but not always accurately as handicapped, were children who spent their formative years (for some 3, for some 8) in an arid and deprived environment. Living conditions provided an absolute minimum of sensory stimulation; the children were physically restrained; social contact was essentially of a functional nature; emotional concern received no consideration; and intellectual development was disregarded. (The children were initially viewed as ineducable). Typically, the children evidenced delayed motor development in fine and gross motor skills; immature and bizarre movement patterns; poor spatial awareness; poor body awareness; and little control over or variety in the quality of movement. There was hunger for contact yet at times fear of contact. There was little evidence of co-operative behaviour; minimal signs of children trusting, caring or turn-taking; eye contact between child and adult and child and child was minimal; and delayed intellectual development was most clearly identified in delayed language development.

The children were in an environment which through its own bleakness and lack of human presence failed to provide much stimulation for developing potential and failed to provide opportunity for children to be the recipients of love and affection. It was an environment which in many ways perpetuated a cultural prejudice - an orphan, often a gypsy child and handicapped. There was such little valuing and little to enhance a positive self-perception. This was an environment that had demolished self-esteem yet, the enhancement of self-esteem should have been a priority.

Given such an environment one might be tempted to ask if any form of stimulation or any form of attention would have benefited the children and effected some change in behavioural response. In part, I'm sure this would have been true: providing sweets satisfied a need and could be used to change behaviour! However, implementing the movement programme was more than providing a temporary satisfaction. It gave us a coherent structure within which to work and consequently a more considered approach to the work. With its obvious concern for the physical and psychological being the Sherborne programme held within its parameters something more than sweets!

The most readily observable change in the children, and greatly influenced I would suggest, by the experiences gained in the movement context, can be seen in the children's ability to interact (relate) and communicate - whether in the more routine activities of the orphanage or in the more 'structured' movement environment. It is this aspect of the SDM that I would like to focus on although in the sequential pattern of delivery the more focussed work on 'relationship play' came later in our delivery.

In the early stages the key focus of delivery was on the physical body, using movement to stimulate an awareness of 'my physical body'; i.e. an awareness of 'my' body, its parts and the whole, an awareness of 'me' in space and gradually an awareness of the colouring or quality of 'my' movement. Stimulating the tactile and kinesthetic senses was a key feature of the work. Whilst using the movement activities one was very aware of physical involvement resulting in a social involvement. Children were encouraged to look and imitate, to listen and respond. Slowly a more conscious awareness of another body seemed to emerge and much time was given to movement experiences that were aimed at helping the children realise the effect of their movement on another person's body.

Returning to the focus on the interactive process... most students of child development will be familiar with the work that has focussed on the way that the child's first relationship develops, benefiting from interaction with its parent or caregiver. Research in this area shows how social interaction is one of the first capabilities that an infant develops. The infant's first contact with the outside world is essentially what the child's caregiver presents to the child. Reflect for a moment on the 'usual' interaction between caregiver and infant. A child is held, rocked, squeezed, tickled, hugged, cuddled, talked to, smiled at, sung too: (not a definitive list). The stimulation is multi-sensory, it is a tactile, visual, auditory and a kinesthetic experience. All such experiences help the child build up its knowledge of the environment, of the world she inhabits, of self, of others. Confidence and trust are developed and understood. At an early stage of development and later in childhood the orphan children were deprived of such experiences. SDM very explicitly addresses these areas of development as situations can be created which focus on the quality of interaction, which are multi-sensory, which aim to build-up personal confidence and a confidence in others. In this interactive context thought is given to the role of the child and caregiver as they interact and relate. Is the child the passive partner or one engaging in a more reciprocal partnership or initiating ideas? We have seen children develop through this relationship scale, moving from either an aggressive or passive presence, through a level where the child will share experience to a level where the child shows awareness of the needs of others.

In this 'relationship play' context, other aspects related to the social development of the child were apparent. For example, an understanding of turn taking seemed to develop; eye-contact, one of the most important areas of communication, was encouraged. In this socially interactive environment all children could participate, all could be successful and all were recipients of non-judgemental teaching.

Initially, many of the children were somewhat aggressive in their response to relationship play and it was as if they longed for physical contact but didn't know what to do once they had received it. Over the years my observations have revealed considerable changes. The emotional reactions tend to be less violent and more discriminating. Children now receive and return care both with an adult and another child. Movement behaviours adapt more readily to different circumstances.

In creating movement situations to enhance social interactions I was also aware of the potential for encouraging the child to develop communication skills. This is a claim made by Sherborne for her movement programme and one I believe my observations of the children's changing behaviour would endorse. I have already referred to the delay in language development where communication tended to be one sided with commands and reprimands being used by adults to control social interaction. But words, though highly significant, are not the only means by which an individual communicates. In the natural course of interaction we all use non-verbal communication - often quite unconsciously; for example, such cues as eye contact, facial expressions, posture, gesture and touch. Each of these cues can be analysed further but it is sufficient, I believe, to say that each is a powerful indicator of emotions and feelings. These cues were missing in the natural make-up of the children and if present there was very little variance.

Within SDM these cues were consciously explored and encouraged. The movement environment made it possible to make something that is normally unconscious into something that is very consciously re-created. The clear evidence of progress in this area is the use of communication cues when the children are engaged in imaginative movement experiences - a very natural development of SDM.

Clearly, changes in the children's behaviour have been witnessed. As I stated at the beginning of this paper I cannot make claims that link these changes solely with the implementation of the SDM programme. What I believe I can adequately claim is that the nature of the experiences which comprise the programme have had a significant effect on the children's self-esteem; that is, the children's awareness of their bodies; the children's ability to relate and communicate; the level of sensitivity they display when working with (partnering) other children; and the greater range of quality (tone, colouring) in movement. Developing confidence has afforded opportunity to engage in imaginative movement activities which have asked the children to share, co-operate, be sensitive to a partner or group, to listen to and to make decisions. Theses are behaviours, designed as movement experiences, which are such an intricate part of SDM. Summarised, they are experiences which are concerned with individual qualities and perceptions; with communication and expression; and with social education. They are experiences designed to bring success.

My experiences over a four year period leave me in no doubt that SDM has a crucial role to play in the rehabilitation process of the Romanian orphan children.

Chapter 16

Working with children who have special needs:
A shared learning experience

Peter Brukenwell

> There is a difference between the way the mind accepts an idea, knowing it
> as a theory or as an action. One is rigid and the other is elastic and supple.
> The object of the work is to teach kinaesthetic awareness; everything else
> must be subordinated to that. Kinaesthetic awareness is our guide in the use
> of the body - the pleasurable experience that makes joy out of movement
> and makes movement into an art. We should not allow the subject matter to
> eclipse the above purpose. The science of movement is mechanical, and does
> not necessarily include kinaesthetic awareness. Scholarship in the science
> of movement can do much, but imagination and perception can do more.
>
> Barbara Clark
> Diary entry, January 1957

I work with several groups of children in two schools that specialise in providing education for youngsters who have multiple learning difficulties. All these groups are mixed in terms of gender, age and ability. Two of them consist entirely of children who have profound and multiple disabilities. It is particularly this aspect of my work I wish to refer to, although the same basic approach and application is used in all groups.

Initially, I found myself feeling both anxious and daunted by the prospect of attempting to explore movement experiences with children who had such restricted abilities. My mind raced ahead, constructing either fantasy success or using a variety of tactics to block out my fears surrounding this unknown. Not surprisingly, the reality bore little resemblance to either my fantasies or fears.

I quickly found that because these children are not explicitly asking for something, I felt the permission to interact with them on many levels, bringing to bear whatever skills I might have to do this. In this way, I now feel a great freedom and a great responsibility. Anything can happen; touching, movement, breathing, shared sounds. It is in my work with these children that I most actively bring together my background in Occupational Therapy (OT), Sherborne Developmental Movement (SDM), Zen and Tai Chi. Within a period of an hour, I may work with the children directly or by supporting the staff who work alongside me, but always attempting to encourage this essential sense of freedom. This freedom comes from within the trust established both in myself and in my relationship with the children. This relationship is in its nature both non- invasive and reciprocal and in this way we support each other as we explore together our movement experiences. Sometimes (usually after the event), I realise that I haven't been able to stay open and present in my relationship to the children. As within this freedom, I also feel a rawness and vulnerability, which as well as being thrilling can also tip me into defensive and controlling behaviour.

In the first school where I began this work, I found myself becoming ever more confused and frustrated with my attempts to create "successful sessions". Increasingly, I lost my motivation and began to look for reasons other than myself to explain this apparent "failure". Finally, after several months, it dawned on me that my need to have some sort of set programme would always be doomed to struggle and conflict. The energy I used to give to the struggle to establish my programme can now be given to more creative pursuits. In this way, the children have taught me an important lesson; to go in as open as possible, to listen to what's happening and what's being offered, as opposed to what I want to happen. With this changed attitude, whatever it is that is going on with the children immediately becomes workable. But this way of working has its price; confrontation with the unknown. However, I have found that if I stay relaxed and present i.e. don't panic, I am able to make as clear and genuine a contact with them as possible. It is from this contact, established through touch and movement and perceived via an "inner listening", that I take my cues. Whatever I might say about my work, I want to make clear and fully own this subjective element and the fact that I understand it only after I do it. In the moment of being with them, I am simply listening for this quality of contact. This is the fundamental principle on which I base my work. In order to actively support this approach, I now structure sessions to allow time to facilitate this process, firstly with myself, then extending this awareness to include the children. Deepening the contact with myself through my increasing awareness of the children creates the safety for the unknown to be present. From this unknown comes forth genuine partnership and the possibility of authentic movement experiences.

Inner Listening

Bowing as I enter the Zendo, I become immediately aware of the atmosphere familiar to serious students of movement anywhere; one of silent attentiveness. It is easy to merge into this atmosphere. We begin to move each in his or her own way. The actions and movement sequences in which we are involved all start simply and build in complexity, but it is not the sequences themselves that are notable. What is notable is that, as we move, our attention is directed again and again toward the inner experience of what we are doing - towards "listening to the body". As we move through a pattern, we are directed to really sense the shifting of weight, allowing one part of the body to lead and the remainder following its rotation. We repeat each pattern several times while being gently encouraged to rest our attention lightly in the process. The instructions make the sequences into a series of meditations, each one sending us deeper into the body. By constantly repeating these simple movements, I gradually become increasingly aware of how I fixate my whole body in order to move one part. Occasionally, I feel my body, when left to itself, not needing to do this. By listening carefully and relaxing my need to control, I can begin to feel what needs to happen in the whole of my body in order that the movement of the part can take place freely. In letting my body make the primary response, I am learning that of course I sometimes need to inhibit, to fixate, but that I do this far too much. Silently, I witness my mind imposing itself inappropriately on my body.

It is this willingness and ability to listen to my own body that provides me with the only solid and reliable place from which to begin my work with the children. If this awareness is not present, then neither am I. Shared movement experiences should, I believe, be constantly created and recreated in an active and dynamic partnership that aims to engage the whole of the child. Therefore, the more fully I am able to be present in the moment of "being-with", rather than "doing-to" the child, the more able she is to be fully engaged with me.

Being Present

In my meditaion practice, the most elusive quality is being present in the moment. Simply focusing on my breath, I strive to be present and constantly see it escaping from my grasp. Thoughts, feelings, body sensations, all tug at my attention as my mind flits endlessly from one to another. Bringing myself into the here and now sounds deceptively easy, but is essentially very difficult. I find myself to be the product of a society that constantly encourages me not to focus on the present. I learnt to be afraid of boredom. Preferring to occupy myself desperately; to do several things simultaneously, I felt better when I was busy. My mind constantly moving, splitting, changing direction. All the while, watching myself with rapt concentration, carefully presenting myself to the world in my search for social acceptability.

In working with the children, my constant need to be self critical and self judging can easily get out of hand. The more anxious I am, the more these qualities come to the fore. My anxiety is fuelled by real fears rooted in my past and those I imagine in the future. When together, this combination can ensure my total inability to be in the present. At times like this, the outer form may present as my simply needing to control an 'uncooperative child' rather than seeing an opportunity for a different form of movement experience to manifest. In this way, I continually fall short of those standards which I set myself in contrasting the present situation with what might have been. In order to stay open and remain present in my relationship with the children, I must simply work to accept how I actually feel rather than how my mind thinks I ought to. I continually find that I have to be willing to give myself permission, not so much to get it wrong, but rather to allow myself not to know. In this way, the anxieties and tensions that would otherwise build within my body are prevented from growing to the point where they block the process. By working to maintain and extend my level of awareness, I can't guarantee that I won't lose it (quite the reverse) but I know when I have. In doing so, I retain an ability to choose, an ability to act rather than react and again gently seek via a shared inner listening that place from which the creative unknown can again produce authentic movement.

Some years ago, when I first began to take Tai Chi classes, what had initially seemed to be simple became frustratingly difficult. I couldn't understand why such simple movements were so hard to remember. My teacher explained it this way - imagine you have a light bulb on the top of your head, he suggested, which lights up every time you are present and goes out every time you go out of your body and as a result out also for the present moment. This happens, he explained, every time I think about the past or the future, every time I indulge myself in fantasy or become so caught up with someone or something else that I lose my own sense of self. How long in a period of one hour (the length of my lesson) did I think the light bulb would be lit up? I thought about this and felt that ten minutes would probably be a generous estimate - no wonder it was hard to remember, I was so seldom there!

Now when I play my Tai Chi, I am aware that those same old tendencies are still there but I no longer choose to invest them with the power I used to. I am more content to stay in the moment as I slowly begin to understand the depth and richness of this place. The outer form of my practice remains basically the same, but my inner perception of the experience constantly changes and deepens. Paradoxically, the more I slow down, the less I do, the more I achieve. The children also teach me this same principle.

Children as Teachers

When I first met Phillip (not his real name), I thought he was about 9 years old - he was in fact 14; his misshapen body gave me few clues to him as a person. Phillip is profoundly and multiply disabled, being unable to speak and requiring total help with all aspects of life. Phillip only has control of his head and to some extent his arms, one of which he uses to indicate yes or no. How I wondered might I explore movement experiences with someone as disabled as Phillip, how could his body with all its limitations be both a source of enjoyment and communication for him? I knew, I thought, how I could include Phillip in group activities with more able children but I wanted him, like them, to as much as possible lead the experience and to have sense of genuine participation and partnership. My mind searched for answers to these questions - none came.

When I actually began to work with Phillip, we started like all sessions, ie, on the floor spending time quietly together using touch and body contact to support a shared inner listening. As Phillip tends to make continual small movements and as these are not generally under his conscious control, this didn't help the process - so I thought. My mind was beginning yet again to get overly caught up with attempting to understand rationally, becoming increasingly 'goal-focused', rather than just being with the process. In this, I could also begin to feel my body becoming as rigid and fixed as Phillip's. It was also apparent that Phillip was not enjoying the process much either; his eyes and body gave me the messages his voice could not. We settled back into the unknown, resting for a while, free of my need to succeed. Slowly and with no help from me (other than getting my mind out of the way), Phillip's inner dance manifested. The deepening quality of contact revealed connections and movements previously hidden to me. Moving through and into this contact, my increasing awareness sensed subtle movement qualities in areas that had previously seemed fixed and rigid. These qualities being both simultaneously separate and yet also part of the whole that is uniquely Phillip. Here was a new world of possibilities for us to explore. As we moved through planes of movement normally denied to Phillip, legs became levers that could easily promote whole body movements, feet became interesting when seen appearing above his head. The deformities of Phillip's spine and ribs created an opportunity to roll and share weight in ways new to us both. Together, we explored the possibilities of movement, becoming bolder, sensing our boundaries of trust and confidence, enjoying this new sense of freedom. Phillip's body and eyes now communicated a different message - one of the ease and contentment that simply comes from movement being experienced in the present moment.

In my initial listening for a movement experience initiated by Phillip, I had imposed a field of reference that made sense to me but not to him. In doing so, I had failed to listen to what he was offering me. His deformed and rigid body spoke of a movement quality so different from my own and yet perfectly able to find its own expression. In the sessions that followed, Phillip has continued to develop further confidence in himself and his body as he learns to initiate more movements for himself. This can take the form of actual movement experiences, or, by communicating more fully his willingness or otherwise to share in the process. Philip also continues to teach me that my frames of reference with regard to movement are far from complete and represent only my reality.

In this way, all the children constantly offer me an opportunity to further question my learnt attitudes and beliefs about functional movement. I seem to live in a culture that holds strict definitions and value judgements about what is seen as moving and not moving. With so much of daily motion and perception dictated by task, function and particular examples of productivity, movement at deeper levels than external appearances are less valued, ignored and at worse, unperceived. How I am seen by others influences my self-image, presence and movement in the world.

The challenge of my work is therefore to create the supportive means both for myself and others to explore and deepen our awareness through movement experiences. While working in this way, the focus is how we make contact with ourselves while touching, supporting and moving with someone who has some needs different from our own. Having established this contact, I also encourage genuine partnership which by its very nature requires mutual dependency and the unknown to be present. This is an environment recognised mainly by trust and intuition, and as such, therefore seldom visited by medical science. The process may appear a risky one, lacking as it does conventional and traditional techniques. Yet, I believe it to be essential if the learning process is to be more than just a mechanical response to the demands of society.